The Negro in the
American Theatre

THE NEGRO

IN THE

AMERICAN

THEATRE

by Edith J. *Juliet* R. *ich* Isaacs

Theatre Arts, Inc., New York, 1947

Follett Book Co.
3.32
1-30-48 fm
3-31-48 fm

To Alain Locke

Because he shares the faith that the arts provide a firm and rewarding two-way passage for men of good will of all races, creeds and cultures, everywhere.

Acknowledgments

My thanks to Theatre Arts magazine, and especially to its editor, Rosamond Gilder, for permission to reprint a part of the material which appeared some years ago in an issue which bore the same title as this book. It was, indeed, the fact that the magazine was sold out three days after it came off the press that induced me to go to work to gather more of the story of the Negro's contribution to the theatre. Since some of the material is not in any printed account that I know of, some of it only in journalistic records which differ considerably among themselves as to names, dates, opinions and even facts, I owe special thanks to many people who have helped me to clarify the story—to Edna Thomas, Carl Van Vechten, Abbie Mitchell, Mercer Cook and Owen Dodson, to Opal Cooper and Frank Wilson who brought me their press books for study and comparison, to Ridgely Torrence who has been generous with his assistance and his files, to the New York Public Library Theatre Collection and Schomburg Collection, to the Museum of The City of New York, and to all the authors, publishers and photographers whose valuable individual contributions are acknowledged as they appear. All Carl Van Vechten's photographs are from the James Weldon Johnson Memorial Collection of Negro Arts and Letters at Yale University or from the Rose McClendon Memorial Collection of Photographs at Howard University Library. My thanks, too, to Richard Harrity who induced me to put the book into shape for publication, to my daughter Hermine Popper, who has a gentle but discerning way of pointing out the flaws in a script and of helping to set them straight, to Robert MacGregor, who put the book through the press. And, of course, to Alain Locke for guidance and for inspiration all along the line.

E. J. R. I.

Contents

Illustrations

ROSE McCLENDON, a gallant artist who through a long career carried her torch high and passed it on to a younger generation when she died in Nineteen Thirty-six.

1

THE BACKGROUND: CHIEFLY BEFORE 1890

LONG BEFORE the Blues came "like a great musical Mississippi, only running North," even before our stages were filled with minstrel shows, born out of plantation playtimes around the Negro cabins, there was a Negro theatre playing the classics in New York City. This theatre itself did not have a very long life, but its influence has passed on through many generations, for, watching its plays with eager attention was a young Negro, Ira Aldridge, who became in his time one of the famous stars of the European theatre.

As early as 1821, this African Company of Negro actors was performing in an improvised playhouse at the corner of Bleecker and Mercer Streets or, as the records put it, "in the rear of the One Mile Stone, Broadway." The One Mile Stone, it is explained, refers to a stone that once stood on the corner of Broadway and Prince Street to mark the distance from City Hall. The African Company's leading player was James Hewlett, who seems to have made his greatest successes as Othello and Richard the Third. Shakespeare was a favorite in the repertory but the company played other classics as well. There was a good-sized and active Negro colony in New York and the audience, though not over-large, was enthusiastic. Unfortunately, white hoodlums filled the empty seats and raised such a rumpus that before long the theatre was closed. But the district in which they played remained for some years the center of life of the New York Negro community. The theatre was not far from Fraunces' Tavern (purchased by the Sons of the Revolution in 1905 as an historic memorial) which had belonged in George Washington's day to Samuel Fraunces, a West Indian Negro. Here Washington often dined, and here he said goodbye to his officers in 1783 at a dinner given in his honor by Governor Clinton. Not far away, too, was the African Free School, which had been started in 1787 and was, a little later, aided by grants from the Corporation of the City. It has been noted as a curious historical fact that the establishment of the African Free School gave Negro children in New York the advantages of such education before it was available to white children.

Out of the Free School came the most remarkable single figure in Negro theatre history, Ira Aldridge. The records of Aldridge's fabulous life are varied, especially as to the early years, but one may accept the version that he was the grandson of a Senegalese chieftain who had, at the suggestion of missionaries, sent his son Daniel, Aldridge's father, to America to be educated for the ministry so as to serve his own people later in Senegal. The chieftain, however, was killed in a tribal war before his son's education was complete. Daniel Aldridge decided to stay in America and became the pastor of a Presbyterian chapel in New York. Ira Aldridge was born in New York about 1807. (Some versions say that he was born in Maryland.) The theatre seems to have fascinated him completely from his earliest years. He played the part of Rolla, the hero in Sheridan's *Pizarro,* in some private theatre, and, soon afterward, he took a job at the Chatham where he could stand behind the scenes every night and watch and listen to the actors. In order to insure him a first-rate education, however, his father sent him to the University of Glasgow where several Negro anti-slavery leaders received their education and where Aldridge is reported to have made an excellent record for himself in his studies. But the hold that the theatre had on him could not be shaken off and before long Aldridge was playing Othello at the Royalty in London. Soon he is reported playing successfully at the Coburg and then at Sadler's Wells. He toured the English provinces and in 1833 played Othello in Covent Garden. His pictures show him to have been a man of fine presence and undoubted grace. And letters and diaries of the period speak of his rich, melodious, almost hypnotic voice. During a Dublin engagement, a little later, Edmund Kean saw Aldridge and engaged him at once to play Othello to Kean's Iago. The two men became fast friends and for two years they played and toured

20

England and the Continent together. Othello seems to have been Ira Aldridge's favored part but he had a large repertory and won distinction as the Moor in *Titus Andronicus* which had not been played in England for 200 years. His acclaim all over England, however, was as nothing to the enthusiasm he aroused on the Continent. He became an intimate friend of Alexandre Dumas, the son of Napoleon's General Dumas, who was himself half Negro. The King of Prussia awarded him the order of Chevalier. The King of Sweden invited him to Stockholm. He was made a member of many learned societies. In St. Petersburg, his performance was a triumph. In the correspondence between Richard Wagner and Mathilde Wesendonck, in the section headed "Zurich, 1853-1858," there appears this note: "For your attention: Wednesday, *Othello*, with Ira Aldridge. Tickets should be secured well in advance."

In 1865, Aldridge went back to London to play Othello at the Haymarket to the Desdemona of Madge Robertson (later Mrs. Kendal) who was then just at the beginning of her great career. From London, he went to Poland for a season and while there died as he was making arrangements for a long-delayed American tour. That was in 1867.

There are stories, not authenticated, of earlier short tours that Aldridge made in America, but his career was not in any sense an integral part of the American Negro theatre. His style, his standards and his success, however, have been a vitalizing influence on Negro actors across both the ocean and the years.

* * * * *

While Ira Aldridge was carrying the banner of Negro acting across the continent of Europe, the Negroes of the Southland sent another form of entertainment North: the minstrel show. But they did not come with it. For many years there were no Negro minstrels in the professional theatre; Mr. Bones, Tambo and their fellows were white men playing in blackface. But the source of their humor and the original pattern of their dance and song, long before it became a caricature of itself, was in the plantations of the deep South.

There is direct evidence of this in the words and music of the songs and the now familiar Negro rhythms of the dances. And more evidence in the paintings of the period. There is, for example, an anonymous watercolor, painted about 1790, and now titled "The Old Plantation," which hangs in Ludwell-Paradise House in Williamsburg, Virginia. It shows a group of Negroes, all rigged up, gathered near a cabin

THE OLD PLANTATION, a watercolor by an unknown artist which hangs now in Ludwell-Paradise House, Williamsburg, Virginia. It shows a group of Negroes who may well be forerunners of the minstrels, dancing and singing to the music of banjo and drum before their cabins. The master's house is dimly seen in the distance.

watching a banjo player, a drummer and a group of dancers. And there are paintings like those of William S. Mount that have lately come to special attention, paintings of singers and dancers and banjo players and especially one called "The Bones Player," a portrait of a man using the actual rib-bones of a sheep, sheared and scraped, like castanets, the very properties from which the original Mr. Bones got his name.

The story of the minstrels is long and gay and changing. It is quite possible that the show-folk from the North who travelled down the Mississippi with their acts saw some of those traveling companies of better plantation minstrels, who were sometimes permitted to carry their acts to their neighbors and even to nearby towns. No doubt, also, plantation owners offered their amusing Negro singers and dancers as entertainment to Northern visitors who carried word of the novelty home. In any case, the first minstrels who played on the professional stage in New York were always white men with their faces covered with burnt cork. As early as 1843, a quartet headed by Dan Emmet, who wrote "Dixie," appeared. They called themselves "The Virginia Minstrels." And the fever spread. For almost fifty years minstrels were the most popular form of American entertainment.

It was only after the end of the Civil War that the Negro himself began to share in the command of the professional minstrel stage. By that time, a regular form for a minstrel show had been completed and its essential elements were maintained over many years. For the first half of the performance a group of at least seventeen men, elaborately costumed, their faces covered with burnt cork, sat in a half-circle. At the center was the interlocutor, the master of ceremonies, who played straight, fed the comedians and was usually the butt of their gay humor. On either side of him were a minimum of seven singers, dancers, monologuists or other featured performers, and at the end of each line the "end men," Mr. Bones and Tambo, named for the instruments they played (bones used like castanets, and a tambourine) who were also the leading comics. The band that supplied the music was either in the pit or behind the circle of actors. The performance always began with the interlocutor's ritual of command: "Gentlemen, be seated," and was followed by ballads, comic songs, humorous dialogues, travestied stump speeches, topical jokes, soft-shoe or buck-and-wing dances, all in quick succession, and by a "walk-around" as the curtain came down. The second half was the "olio," less traditional in form and more like

23

From James Bland, E. B. Marks Music Corp.

THE LINE-UP of The Georgia Minstrels showing the end-men, Mr. Bones and Tambo, and the interlocutor in the center, on what was probably a poster or music cover.

24

a later burlesque or vaudeville show with sketches, except that the players were—as in Shakespeare's theatre—all males, with the Negro "wenches" a much sought-for solo part for a character actor.

When Negroes were admitted to the professional stage they took over bodily the entire minstrel convention, even to the use of burnt cork and the thickened lips. It was an imitation of an imitation of the plantation life of their fellows. But Negro singers and composers, and especially Negro dancers, gave new life to the form and many of their companies prospered. There are certain names that stand out among all accounts of the Negro performers: Billy Kersands, a dancer, the Bohee brothers, who sang and played the banjo as accompaniment to a certain soft-shoe dance which was their specialty, Sam Lucas and James Bland. Bland shares with Stephen Foster the title of master among "sweet minstrels," the writers and singers of romantic ballads as opposed to the composers of the livelier, jig rhythms.

It is interesting that neither Bland nor Foster, who added so many songs of the Southland to our permanent American repertory, was born or bred in the South. Foster, son of a mayor of Pittsburgh, whose most popular and successful days were in the 50's, a little ahead of Bland, lived for a time in Cincinnati and often crossed over the river to visit relatives in Kentucky where there were plenty of plantation singers to listen to. That seems to be as far South as he ever went. Most Americans would probably know that Stephen Foster wrote "Swanee River" (he wrote this and many more of his best songs for Cristy's Minstrels), "Old Black Joe" and "My Old Kentucky Home." But there are few who would know who composed "Carry Me Back to Ole Virginny," "In the Morning by the Bright Light," "In the Evening by the Moonlight," which were among the most popular of the countless songs by James Bland, probably the most talented and versatile star of minstrelsy in its best days. Bland was born on Long Island, of Negro, white, and Indian parentage, not far from where William Mount painted his Negro folk scenes. In search of an education, he got as far as Howard University in Washington when the urge toward music was too strong and he ran away with his banjo under his arm to join Callender's Minstrels in their tour of the country.

Far too little is known of James Bland and his music. It is not because his work was that of a Negro that it has been neglected but chiefly for two reasons that have little to do with race. The first was the mat-

25

ter of our lax copyright laws and the low level on which most music business was transacted in those days. The second was the carelessness and the profligacy of the musicians themselves. But the Negro, especially a man of unusual and virtuoso talents, like Bland, suffered in addition from one of his own virtues. Like many Negro musicians today, he could extemporize so brilliantly that it was almost impossible to write down the music of his songs as he played and sang them himself.

Many of the same things that happened to Bland happened to Stephen Foster. He, too, in spite of his background, was a brilliant but "irresponsible troubadour." Only recently a writer, delving into some old Pittsburgh records, found a newspaper account of a newly performed opera in which the librettist was treated with dignity and scope, but the musician was only mentioned and named as "one Stephen Foster." No doubt Foster, as an individual, also suffered from much the same business chicanery that Bland did. But there was a marked difference in the result of their treatment because the Negroes were just beginning to establish themselves in the public mind as creative artists, even on the level of popular songs. And they could not, as a race, afford to lose the credit due to work as good as that of James Bland.

At one period, the history of minstrelsy ran parallel to the main road of the American theatre. A Negro named Charles Hicks, in 1865, organized an all-Negro company that he called The Georgia Minstrels. They included a group of trained musicians who played well enough to attract an audience to concert halls. Hicks was a good director and manager, but he had more than his share of trouble carrying his company through the South and Charles Callender took it over. A little later he made Gustave Frohman, older brother of Charles and Daniel, his advance agent and then manager. When Gustave moved up, Daniel moved in. When Gustave later started a comedy company of his own, he gave Charles the job of advance agent. Jack Haverly bought the minstrel company and took them to Europe as Haverly's European Minstrels, headed by Billy Kersands and Sam Lucas. To the other big names in the troupe were added the Bohee brothers and James Bland. In 1882, Charles Frohman bought the company and brought them back, touring them again under the name of Callender's Consolidated Spectacular Colored Minstrels. In these lively days, several well-known Negro companies were also running successfully and in 1893, Primrose and West sent out the first mixed troupe which they called The Forty

Whites and Thirty Blacks. One other note about the Frohmans. Once when their comedy company was stranded, Gustave had an idea which was generally considered to be an inspiration. Since 1852 there had hardly been a time when *Uncle Tom's Cabin*, with a white company, had not been played somewhere in cities, towns or rural districts. Now Gustave telegraphed to his brother: "Get me an Eva and send her down with Sam Lucas." So Lucas became the first Negro to play Uncle Tom.

Minstrelsy, as a theatre form, is gone today, perhaps never to return, and it may be just as well. There is little doubt that it helped to create and to fix the Negro stereotypes—passive or scheming, over-dull or over-shrewd, but always irresponsible and caricatured—which have burdened our theatre ever since. Yet it was our first authentic American theatre form. It left us the vaudeville monologue, many dance routines, the double forms of music that Isaac Goldberg calls "music of the heels" and "music of the heart." And it trained many of the next generation of Negro singers, dancers, composers and comedians.

Harvard Library Theatre Collection

JAMES BLAND, *surrounded by some of the characters in his songs that the whole country learned from the minstrels.*

2

THE MIDDLE DISTANCE: 1890-1917

New York was inching up, inching northward, away from the Battery to Washington Square, up to 20th street and into the 30's, always a little closer to Central Park, then east and west of the Park and on toward Harlem. Many New York Negroes, especially the wealthier and more sedate families, had left New York and established themselves in Brooklyn where they owned their own homes and developed a business and social life of their own. Many others moved to Washington and Philadelphia and other cities where Negro colleges were growing in stature and in size. But as the center of New York life shifted, a large group of Negroes moved with it, usually around the fringes of the neighborhoods that many of them now served as small tradesmen, entertainers, band leaders and musicians, caterers, etc. And as the narrow island began to narrow down its dwelling spaces, men began, as they often do in tight, urban communities, more and more to seek relaxation in their clubs and lodges and saloons. New York Negroes were especially devoted to their clubs which had a pattern of their own and which probably set the pattern for the major features of today's night clubs. There was almost always a restaurant, sometimes a bar, with or without a license. On an upper floor there were usually small rooms for private parties or card games or meetings, and a "back room" where musicians, actors and dancers could practice their sketches and routines. On the "parlor floor" there was a large room with small tables at the side, a piano, and a clear space in the center for dancing by the guests, or by special performers.

By 1900, the Hotel Marshall on West 53rd Street was a highspot among Negro meeting places. It became a favorite of the successful Negro theatre artists of the day. By that time, too, many New York Negroes had money to spend, and they spent it freely. In the world of sports, especially as jockeys and in the prize ring, Negroes were tops. Thirteen out of the fourteen jockeys who rode in the first Kentucky Derby were Negroes. These heroes of the stage and track and their fellows of the prize ring were the center of attraction not only for Negroes but for many other New Yorkers, who liked to admire and come close to their popular favorites and who liked the sound of Negro music and talk. And they had a special attraction for the theatre folk who were playing in blackface and liked to see the types they represented, or the Negro artists they imitated, in the flesh.

This whole group was of course a very small segment of Negro life in America, even in New York. For by that time, only forty-five years after emancipation, the American Negro had cut down his illiteracy over fifty percent, had educated fifty thousand ministers, teachers, doctors, lawyers, editors, authors, architects and engineers, many of them in European universities as well as in the colleges of the North and West. Negro inventors had taken out four hundred patents. Several of their own colleges were building up fine records and graduating men of quality who became leaders of their people in many fields.

That is the racial background for the pleasant, but still limited, field of the Negro in the theatre at the turn of the century. These were the years when Edwin Booth was still revered as master of the art of acting, when the plays of Clyde Fitch and Eugene Walter and David Belasco held sway and *The Great Divide* gave a poet (William Vaughn Moody) a first opportunity to pit the great open spaces of the West against New England as play material. They were the years of the lush musicals— of George Lederer and Charles Dillingham and especially of Florenz Ziegfeld and the glorified American girl.

For the Negroes the years from 1890-1917 were the years of the cakewalk and the "coon songs," the Jonah Man and the beginnings of ragtime. But they were also the days when the Spirituals came to be appreciated as music, when the South began to loose the flood of the

29

ERNEST HOGAN (at left, with Carita Day) was one of the most important of the early Negro comedians. A fluent and popular composer as well as an excellent singer and actor, he developed the characters of Rufus Rastus and The Oyster Man. He is credited with having changed the comic tradition from the "silly end-man into a character with a slight, very slight, quality of the Harlequin." He toured the country with the so-called "Black Patti," Sissieretta Jones, who headed the first important Negro musical organization to tour both North and South successfully.

BOB COLE (standing, right, with J. Rosamond Johnson at the piano) was, for many years, the head of Worth's Museum, the center of Negro theatrical activity in New York. He not only directed the shows there, but wrote many of them—words, lyrics and music—and acted, danced and sang in them when that was needed. Later, teamed with J. Rosamond Johnson, he wrote the first true Negro operettas, *A Trip to Coontown, The Shoofly Regiment, Red Moon*. He was still a very young man and at the height of his creative ability when he died. To Johnson we owe, among other good things, many of the best versions of Negro Spirituals.

Blues, when the Negro was gradually to slough off the caricature of himself in blackface and to try his hand at serious playwriting and composition. There were many gifted men among the comedians, the dancers, the composers of these earlier days.

Not much is left in actual performance of the things that were then most popular, but, on the other hand, almost everything that Negro theatre artists and musicians are doing today had its beginnings in the Middle Distance and much of what our theatres and concert halls and radio, and most of what our night clubs are doing had its source or its flood-tide here.

A change may be said to have begun when Sam Jack, manager of a burlesque circuit, decided to arrange a complete show with Negro performers. *The Creole Show* was planned on the general pattern of the minstrels with one major innovation. It featured a chorus of sixteen beautiful Negro girls who sang and danced. The show opened in Boston in 1891, went on to Chicago and played at Sam Jack's Opera House there during the entire season of the World's Fair. For five years, in one form or another, *The Creole Show* went on. Then in 1895, John W. Isham, a Negro who had been advance agent for *The Creole Show*, decided to establish himself as a producer with a show called *The Octoroons*. This was somewhat further from the minstrel pattern, and Isham's next production, *Oriental America*, ended not with a cakewalk and a walkaround in the traditional manner, but with an operatic medley. The importance of this feature was not so much the music as the musicians. For instead of the established burlesque performer, Mr. Isham engaged Sidney Woodward, a fine tenor who had already made a reputation in Boston, J. Rosamond Johnson and Inez Clough, of whom much was to be heard in the theatre—Negro and white—for many years. *Oriental America* broke another important precedent by playing, not at a burlesque house, but at Palmer's Theatre, later called Wallack's.

By this time Negroes in New York were more active in the theatre than they had ever been before. Worth's Museum on Sixth Avenue and Thirtieth Street had become a Negro stock theatre with a full company of players and a group of apprentices who were having their first opportunity for training. For some time the company was headed by Bob Cole, a young man well-educated and deeply concerned with the dignity of his profession. He was a good singer and dancer, an excellent actor. He could write an entire show: dialogue, lyrics and music. He staged his own musical shows and acted in some of them. Moreover, Cole was often engaged on major projects for other managers. One of these projects was *Black Patti's Troubadours*. Black Patti was a singer named Sissieretta Jones who had carried off high honors in the concert field. Her manager believed that a show with an operatic finale, in which Black Patti appeared with the chorus, would be a success, and he was right. The show which Bob Cole wrote for her played for many years all the way from Proctor's 58th Street Theatre in New York through the larger cities of the North and then through the South. It was the only one of the large Negro shows to play the South successfully in those days.

In 1898, Bob Cole wrote *A Trip to Coontown,* a musical with a plot that made the break with minstrel technique complete. Whenever he was not engaged in regular theatre work of one kind or another, he was a member of one of the most popular vaudeville teams of the time, Cole and Johnson. His first Johnson partner was Bill Johnson; later he was teamed with J. Rosamond Johnson who was already making a name for himself in various branches of music. With J. Rosamond, Cole wrote the first true Negro operettas, *The Shoofly Regiment* and *Red Moon.* Bob Cole's death, while he was still a very young man, was a great loss to the whole Negro theatre movement.

Things seemed to happen quickly in the 90's; more opportunities opened up after each success. Each time, too, musicians were less afraid to provide shows with their best music, and librettists began to offer more variety. In 1898 Will Marion Cook, trained under Joachim in Europe, wrote a sketch called *Clorindy: The Origin of the Cakewalk,* which gave a clear indication of a fresh and genuine musical talent. It also, for the first time, showed what syncopation could be like in gifted hands. The lyrics were by the poet Paul Laurence Dunbar, and the sketch, which ran through a whole summer with Cook directing the orchestra, was produced by one of New York's leading musical producers, George W. Lederer, at the Casino Roof Garden. Featured in the cast was a favorite minstrel, Ernest Hogan, creator of *Rufus Rastus* and *The Oyster Man,* a natural pantomimist, who stands near the head of the line of Negro comics.

To Bert Williams, just coming into his own at that time, is generally conceded "top-top" place in the field, by his own people, by

32

dramatic critics, by the men with whom he worked in vaudeville, in his own companies and in the *Follies*. Nobody ever called Egbert Austin Williams anything but Bert Williams unless they called him Shakespeare's "humorous man," or the "son of laughter." W. C. Fields spoke of him as: "the funniest man I ever saw; the saddest man I ever knew."

The story of Bert Williams' life is in so many ways the epitome of the Negro artist's story that it seems worth telling here in some detail, much of which comes from a friendly book edited, after his death, by Mabel Rowland.

Williams' grandfather, a white man, was the Danish Consul in Antigua in the West Indies. He owned a big plantation where Bert spent his youngest years, watching the ships that one branch of his family owned put out from the harbor laden with the rum that was distilled and exported by another branch of the family. Bert Williams' grandmother, a native of the island, was three-fourths Spanish and one-fourth African. His father married a quadroon who was the sister of the Church of England clergyman in Antigua. Life started gaily enough but soon Bert's father was taken ill. The family fortune vanished all too quickly and the island physician recommended a move to California for the father's health. There Bert went to school, looked longingly at Leland Stanford University and knew that there would never again be money enough in the family till to enable him to pass those magic gates.

But books, especially philosophy, were his close companions all his life. They kept him, as he said, "in harmony." Later when the days were dark, spiritually, he spent long hours in his library at home, night after night. And when he died, there were, among his favorite books, well-worn volumes of Tom Paine, Confucius, Schopenhauer, Goethe, Voltaire and Mark Twain.

From his earliest youth, Bert Williams was a natural singer and could play enough on almost any instrument to get by. He had also a great gift for mimicry and an eager interest in developing this raw talent into an art. His eyes and ears were always open. He watched every bird and every animal he saw. He made mental notes of the movement and the speech of every kind of man and boy he met. With this equipment and a banjo in his hand he started out to make a living at the cafes and honkytonks of San Francisco. At one of these he met a "tramp" player, also a Negro, by the name of George Walker, who was obviously a

THE STARS of *In Dahomey* do a "walk around," with Hattie MacIntosh leading, followed by George Walker, Ada Overton Walker, Bert Williams and Lottie Williams. In the early 1900's even the most successful plays did not have the long runs they do today. Yet *In Dahomey* managed somehow to make an international name for itself and its players and to go from Broadway to a year's triumphal run in London.

man of more than usual comic gifts. The two decided to set out as a team, Walker to dance and play the stooge, Williams the straight man and singer. Before they achieved their major success on the professional stage, however, these characters had been reversed, a tribute to their art.

Every trick of voice, inflection and gesture that Williams used in the theatre was learned by careful study and observation. He was, by nature, a tall, straight, handsome man with no trace in his English even of the vernacular of his homeland. Yet, in the theatre, playing in blackface, Williams was the slouching, lazy, careless, unlucky Negro for whom everything went wrong. His dialect was so perfect that it became the type for low-grade Negro speech much as Amos 'n Andy used it yesterday. Walker was the dandy, the sporting Negro, dressed a little too high, spending generously whatever he was able to borrow or filch from the Jonah Man's hard-earned money.

Williams and Walker had the usual up-hill work before they had their first big success at Koster and Bial's. It was almost as much a surprise to them as to anyone when from the very first night the audience went wild about them. They remained at that house for twenty-eight weeks, establishing a record. The team's first successful starring venture was in a show of their own called *The Sons of Ham,* which played for two years. It was in this that Williams, collaborating with Alex Rogers, wrote the song "I'm a Jonah Man," which suited his personality so well that he was never afterward permitted by his audience to escape entirely from the character. The Jonah Man represented the mournful and melancholy, quaint and philosophical, but exceedingly funny fellow, with the discouraged shoulders, the shambling gait and the stumbling dialect of the ignorant Southern Negro.

A little later Williams and Walker presented *In Dahomey* at the New York Theatre on Broadway and they played to jammed houses. Arriving on Broadway was a triumph in itself. Yet the "Theatre Magazine" said, and undoubtedly correctly, "there is nothing very artistic or remarkable about *In Dahomey.* It is on the same level with the average Broadway musical comedy, but thanks to Mr. Williams it is a good deal more diverting."

With only that recommendation and not even a long run to go on, the next chapter of *In Dahomey's* history becomes even more remarkable. England, at that time, liked American shows that caricatured

ABBIE MITCHELL, the little girl with a voice of rare beauty who came from a Baltimore convent to audition for Will Marion Cook's *Clorindy*. At fourteen she took over the lead in the musical (as shown here) and married the composer. Later she studied with Jean de Reszke, toured America and Europe in musical plays and concerts and gave three command performances for two Kings of England. Soon she developed into a dramatic as well as a singing actress. She played leads in many of the Williams and Walker shows and became one of the chief attractions of Harlem's Lafayette Theatre, where she sang the leading roles in *Carmen* and *Traviata* and starred in many dramas. The critic of "The New York Sun" said, "Her voice is one of the most beautiful heard this season. And her stage presence bespeaks the singer to the manner born." In the Twenties she was seen in *In Abraham's Bosom* (see page 81), and more recently she is known for parts like Clara in *Porgy and Bess* and Addie in *The Little Foxes*.

America, in one way or another, better than she liked our serious plays. So in 1903 Hurtig and Seamon, the managers, decided to take *In Dahomey* to London. Williams and Walker had failed in a vaudeville engagement in England some years earlier and they dreaded the prospect of a return. When the play got started at the Shaftesbury Theatre and met with only moderate favor they were sure their fears were justified. But for some reason the man who arranged command performances at Buckingham Palace decided that he wanted *In Dahomey* for the birthday celebration of the young Prince of Wales. The story of what happened then is surely as funny as any of the Williams and Walker scripts.

The birthday celebration was a great event, of course. A theatre in the garden was erected for the occasion with a large stage, a fly gallery and full lighting equipment. Jesse Shipp, co-author, co-actor and stage director, was still fussing about with costumes and properties when Bert Williams arrived on the scene late in the day. Shipp had been at it hard from early morning and he declared that everything was ready— or would have been—if too many people from the palace had not come down to ask questions. He said that he had kept his temper as long as he could, but finally, when a stout gentleman in a red vest asked if he found anything wrong with the English way of doing things, he "let that fellow have it." He told him everything that was wrong, emphasizing especially the difference between porter service at London's railway stations and at Grand Central in New York. The man, he said, didn't seem to mind.

In the evening the curtain was still down when the strains of "God Save the King" filled the air and the Royal Family and their party came down the steps and into the garden. All the peepholes in the curtain (and several newly made) had eyes glued to them. "Lemme see the King," said Shipp grouchily. They showed him the central figure and he gasped, "That man! My God, the fat man with the red vest! I was looking for a King to look like a King!"

The King himself, when he and Williams were later on friendly terms, laughed incontinently at this story. And Williams' comment was "I was grateful that the thing had happened to a monarch with such a sense of humor, that we were not in Georgia, say, or Texas under similar circumstances."

Bert Williams and his company became the rage of London. Night after night for months the theatre was full. There were other command performances. All fashionable London was cakewalking and doing the buck-and-wing. Distinguished artists, scholars, politicians took Williams to their clubs and to their homes.

After London, the *In Dahomey* company toured the provinces and Scotland, and in Edinburgh Williams and several others of the company were invited to become Masons, joining Waverly Lodge #597, an association which meant a great deal to Bert Williams. It was only when he came back to America that he said, "It is no disgrace to be a Negro but it is very inconvenient."

Abyssinia was the next Williams and Walker venture, and was followed by another on the same model, *Bandana Land*. For most of these big shows, Will Marion Cook and Will Vodery were the chief composers and arrangers of the music. Alex Rogers was the chief librettist; Jesse Shipp, the chief stage manager; Ada Overton Walker, Stella Wiley, Hattie MacIntosh were leading women players. But actors, managers, musicians, directors all did many other things beside their specialty and —sooner or later—almost every Negro actor, dancer and composer drifted into the Williams and Walker company for one of the big popular shows. The team was at the top of its favor when illness cut short Walker's career and soon, for the second time, death carried off a talented young Negro actor. For a while Bert Williams was almost unable to carry on without his partner. The music in their shows had, it is true, been improving steadily. But the special vein of humor that was the basis of their librettos was running thin. Nobody knew this better than Bert Williams. Perhaps too, he was beginning to be conscious of an increasing envy, in the world of the theatre, of the success of Negro musicals. Anyhow, at about this time, two important things happened.

Bert Williams, instead of continuing his own shows, joined the *Follies* at the invitation of Abraham Erlanger. That was in 1910 and was considered a great opportunity. Williams was given every chance —within the limit of low comedy—and he was an instantaneous hit. He was popular with other players and his popularity with the public grew year by year, but he was never happy in his work. Ring Lardner knew at least one reason why: "The men who wrote the old Williams and Walker shows knew how to write for Bert. The *Follies* people don't." Williams wanted to do a serious play and several critics, as well as other actors, were sure that he could master many fine roles. His contract with

38

WILLIAMS AND WALKER in *Abyssinia*. Bert Williams played his typical role of the dull-witted, lazy, unlucky, uneducated Negro who always managed by some stroke of extraordinary stupidity to make the best-laid plans go wrong. This "Jonah Man" was a masterpiece of acting, for nothing could have been more unlike Bert Williams in his real-life appearance and character. There are still many people who remember the "lies" which were always a loudly applauded part of Williams' act, and there are still a few fortunate men who remember how, when Williams came into a crowded parlor or clubroom, somebody would invariably shout: "Bert, tell us a story." He would look around, ask quietly, "Are we all Negroes here?" and then begin a stream of tall tales to the steady accompaniment of chuckles and laughter.

the *Follies* was for three years only and just before the end of that time, David Belasco sent for him to ask if he would not like to act in a play written especially for him, under Belasco's auspices. To Williams this was the happiest moment in his life. It was a great temptation, a great opportunity. But Williams felt that he owed allegiance to *The Follies* (Erlanger and then Ziegfeld) who were the first to give a Negro actor a featured place in a white company. "We've got our foot in the door," he used to say, "we mustn't let it close again." So, for his race's sake, he stayed with *The Follies* for nearly ten years.

He was able, while he was there, to make extraordinarily good use of his rare gift of pantomime. At his pantomime dinner party you could almost taste the food, and in the poker game his facial expression was so remarkable that you could tell what cards each player held, how the bets stood and who won. Also, he perfected the art of the vaudeville monologue and many of his stories, which he called his "lies," are in the repertory of story-tellers today. But nobody has yet matched Bert Williams' slow, restrained, and yet ardent and intensely comic technique. Everyone who ever heard him tell Martin's story, which was in his richest vein, laughs when he speaks of it.

It was a tale about an old Negro preacher who had made himself at home in a haunted house. He was sitting, Bible in hand, drowsing before an open coal fire. Suddenly a cat, a little friendly animal, came down the chimney and started eating the live coals. Soon it was followed by a great big cat who, after it had its feed of coals, asked: "When we gwine begin?" The first cat answered, "We can't do nothin' till Martin comes." One after another the cats came, each larger than the last. Each ate its fill and asked, more and more querulously, "When we gwine begin?" Together all the other cats would answer gloomily, "We can't do nothin' till Martin comes." Finally the frightened preacher rose and, rushing out, called back: "When Martin comes, you tell him I was here, but I done gone."

"Of course," Heywood Broun said, "we laughed at the message which was left for Martin. But it was more or less defensive laughter, because we knew in our heart that the preacher had outstayed us by at least one cat. Bert Williams did not tell the story as a comic anecdote. By voice and pantomime, he lifted it to the stature of a true ghost story. We could see the old Negro feverishly turning the pages of the Bible. The cats from the fireplace took form before our eyes. Sparks

40

dripped from their jaws and wind howled outside the cabin. All this was built for us by a tall man, his face clownishly blackened with burnt cork, who stood still, in the center of the stage and used no gesture which travelled more than six inches."

It was not only the audiences and the other actors who applauded Bert Williams. He found almost universal favor with first-line critics, but Broun seemed to have a gift for analyzing his peculiar talent:

"One or two other people in *The Follies* have managed to slosh their way through the lush Urban jungles. Eddie Cantor did it—but Cantor's style of comedy has none of the subtlety which belonged to Williams at his best. The secret of Cantor's appeal lies almost wholly in pace. He goes after a joke as if he were a substitute guard tackling a dummy for the benefit of the head coach. . . .

"There is the same quality of *excitement*, to an even greater degree, in the work of Al Jolson, and Billy Sunday has it. Any one of these three fairly *worries* a spectator into laughing. There is an awesome vitality in this, but we are not sure that it is exactly art. There is too much efficiency in it.

"The old Bert Williams gave you more quiet and consolation. Bert Williams found prosperity and success in the theatre but his high talents were largely wasted. . . . Every round of laughter bound him more securely to his estate as merrymaker. Somehow or other laughing at Bert Williams came to be tied up in people's minds with liberalism, charity and the Thirteenth Amendment."

When Bert Williams left the *Follies*, he was engaged by George Le Maire for *Broadway Brevities*, a revue at the Winter Garden. For the first time he had a salary measured by his drawing power and he had his name in electric lights. Later the Shuberts engaged him for a lead in *Under the Bamboo Tree*, a musical comedy with music by Sigmund Romberg and Will Vodery, with book and lyrics by Walter De Leon. Williams was the star of the show in a company that was otherwise entirely white. Everything was going well in Chicago, but Williams was a sick man and before long was taken home to die, at 46. His funeral was in the Masonic Temple where over 5,000 people paid him the last honors.

Life bore heavily on Williams. His mind was too keen, his soul too sensitive to carry without effect the burden of prejudice and mis-understanding and envy which closed in on him. Even certain men of his own race were not free from resentment. Some of them were plainly envious; others, probably sincere but misunderstanding his motives, felt that he had deserted the Negro theatre for the white theatre when the Negroes most needed him as a leader. But Negroes like Charles Anderson, Collector of the Port of New York, appreciated Williams' personal sacrifice. "His services to the race," Anderson said, "were great and multiple. He blazed a pathway from the minstrel house to the legitimate theatre: he unlocked the door, which had, for centuries, shut out colored performers from white shows. He lessened discrimination by conquering the prejudice of managers and producers. He overcame much of the hostility of the press against mixed casts and he reformed and refined the art, so called, of the (white) black-face comedians, by teaching them to substitute drollery and repose for roughness."

And Booker Washington understood. He said, "Bert Williams has done more for the race than I have. He has smiled his way into people's hearts. I have been obliged to *fight* my way."

THE CAKEWALK, *one of the first Negro dances to sweep the country.*

3

HARLEM: AN INTERLUDE

By 1910 there were almost 100,000 Negroes in the city of New York, over half of them in Manhattan. A small group, descendants of the early settlers, still remained firmly entrenched in their Greenwich Village homes; quite a colony stayed in the 50's and 60's on the West Side. But the trek was to Harlem where an active community was rapidly evolving and calling loudly for a theatre of its own. There was plenty of reason for this. Edward Sheldon's melodrama, *The Nigger,* which had recently been produced at the New Theatre, probably brought the matter to a head. It was one of the major successes of the New Theatre's season, with Annie Russell, Guy Bates Post, and Pedro de Cordoba in the distinguished cast. The newspapers were full of it. The play's theme—considered bold in its day—was a familiar problem, and Sheldon's dramatic intention was sympathetic. He had none of the racial prejudice, none of the "large, natural endowment of malignancy" which so obsessed Thomas Dixon, author of *The Clansman,* a dramatization of which had besmirched the theatre a few years earlier.

Sheldon's hero, Philip Morrow, is an aristocratic, successful Southern politician, who had first been elected to office, as sheriff, on his promise to "keep the niggers in their place." Now, as governor, he is confronted with violent race-riots, which he believes are incited by too much bad whisky. He is urging a law to prohibit the sale of liquor in the state when a cousin—an unscrupulous distiller whom such a law

43

would bankrupt—tells Philip that his grandmother was a beautiful quadroon and that he will announce this to the world and ruin Philip if he persists. Beaten either way, Philip decides to renounce his governorship and to devote the rest of his life to aiding the Negroes of the state.

The characters were well conceived, the action was swift, the climaxes good, and, as melodramas go, the motives and the situations held water. Yet the Negroes were not the only people whom *The Nigger* offended deeply.

There were no Negroes in the New Theatre cast and Negroes were not welcomed in the audience. There was no New York statute against Negroes in theatres, but there was a tradition that barred them almost as effectually as laws from playhouses. Negro playwrights thus had no opportunity to learn the techniques of playwriting. There were Negro characters in many plays and had been from the days of Zeke (1845) in Mrs. Mowatt's *Fashion*; in fact, long before that. But the characters were stereotypes—the comic Negro, the contented slave, the beautiful octoroon, or, like Philip Morrow, a man hounded by his blood. And usually the parts were played by white men, Negro actors being limited to low comedy roles.

There was a young dramatic critic on "The New York Age," one of Harlem's leading newspapers, who resented this situation. His desire was to give Harlem a first-class Negro stock company playing original dramas of Negro life, musicals, and Broadway successes that Negroes never saw. The critic (whose name, by the way, was Lester Walton, until recently our minister to Liberia) leased the Lafayette theatre for his venture. He made it a producing playhouse with a permanent company, many of whom had played in the Cole and Johnson or Williams and Walker shows and many of whom, including Charles Gilpin (soon to be famous as The Emperor Jones) had had years of training at an older Negro theatre, the Pekin in Chicago. At the Lafayette, they played Negro comedy with song and dance. They had a season of grand opera. They played *The Servant in the House, the Thirteenth Chair, The Count of Monte Cristo, Dr. Jekyll and Mr. Hyde, Madame X, On Trial, Within the Law, Paid in Full, Potash and Perlmutter*, and other plays of that caliber. That critical curmudgeon, George Jean Nathan, is authority for the fact that a notable offering of the Shakespeare Tercentenary was the Lafayette *Othello*, with E. S. Wright and Margaret Brown.

44

For some time the Lafayette was highly successful. With its profits it was able to start touring and other producing companies. Its success gave impetus to other producers—Irving Miller, the Tutt Brothers (Whitney and J. Homer), S. H. Dudley—who would take a promising play on tour through such Negro theatres as the Howard in Washington, the Dunbar in Philadelphia. It also encouraged the organization of another important Harlem theatre, the Lincoln. But theatre costs, always high, were growing higher and the taste of the audience was as unstable as it is on Broadway. At first it enjoyed seeing the plays which Broadway liked. But, gradually, a large part of the Harlem audience reverted to its preference for comedy with music, or for melodrama.

There were few good serious plays of Negro life and these did not interest a large enough public to make the theatre pay. Moreover, opinion about the level of the acting showed a wide range. Negro comedy, it was generally agreed, was better than ever. But the actors were inclined to "ham" in the Broadway plays, and the audience was canny enough to know the difference between real acting, as in comedy, and the imitations in *Dr. Jekyll* and *The Thirteenth Chair*, especially since shoddy make-up did not add to the illusion.

Progressive critics, who wished the Negro's theatre ventures to succeed, complained that although there were theatres owned and operated by and for Negroes in New York, Chicago, New Orleans, Jackson, Memphis, Atlanta, Columbus, O., Jacksonville, Fla., Yazoo City, Baton Rouge and Plaquemine, La., they all seemed to be devoted to imitating the white man's stage and the white man's acting instead of developing a drama of their own.

So the Lafayette, as well as the other Harlem theatres, would be prosperous one year and broke the next. Sometimes their spirits lagged, but there seemed always to be a friend to revive their hopes and a patron—or a comedy team—to replenish their bank accounts. And gradually, free from white producers' preferences and social taboos and playing to audiences who understood their racial and emotional reactions, with a permanent company working together week by week, they developed actors who were soon to show their skill elsewhere.

When J. Leubrie Hill, chief director at the Lafayette, staged a jolly show called *The Darktown Follies*, scouts from Broadway heard that something good was going on and came up to see for themselves and, incidentally, to carry away a few ideas. Among the visitors was Florenz

Ziegfeld, who bought the finale for his own use. As the news spread, the white invasion of Harlem's entertainment spots started in earnest. Money rolled in and in 1915 there was, as might have been expected, another show in the same spirit called *Darkydom,* starring the comedians Miller and Lyles, with music by Will Marion Cook, Abbie Mitchell as the leading player and a young night club singer, Opal Cooper, as the tenor. "The New York Age" wrote that the audience on the opening night was reminiscent of Broadway. The Manhattan box parties and the long line of "carriage trade" that had begun with *The Darktown Follies* was doubled. The play went on to capacity houses. But its players and composers were lured to other fields, one at a time; bit by bit, its sketches were bought for Broadway shows. Not until the days of the Federal Theatre did opportunity knock again at Harlem's door in the same genial way.

*   *   *   *   *

While all this was going on, there were important developments in Negro music that very soon began to exert a different, but compelling, influence on the theatre in a variety of ways. "In New York between 1905 and 1912 or 15," Alain Locke says,* "four Negro conductors and arrangers of genius organized Negro music out of a broken, musically illiterate dialect and made it a national and international music with its own peculiar idioms of harmony, instrumentation and technical style of playing. . . .

"Their names? Ford Dabney, James Reese Europe, Will Marion Cook and W. C. Handy. Dabney revolutionized the Negro dance orchestra and started the musical fortunes of Florenz Ziegfeld when he was experimenting with roof-garden shows. Jim Europe, a member of the *Memphis Students,* alternated with Cook as musical director of the Cole and Johnson shows, organized the famous "Clef Club Orchestra" and music center in 1910. Later Europe was to vindicate Negro music in two other ways—to make it preferred for rhythm and accord in the new dance vogue of the American stage started by . . . Vernon and Irene Castle (who insisted on Negro orchestras for their accompanists) and by the still more important vogue for Negro music which Jim Europe started abroad by the uniqueness of the 15th Regiment (367 U. S. Infantry Band) which he organized and led during the War, 1917-18. . . . Will Marion Cook not only gave Negro music its first serious orchestral ambitions, but with his 'syncopated orchestra' sur-

*From "The Negro and His Music," by Alain Locke. By permission of the author.

W. C. HANDY'S songs, beginning with the "Memphis Blues" and the "Saint Louis Blues," are sung from coast to coast, north to south. And fortunately he has taken time out to tell the dramatic story of his life, which he calls "The Father of the Blues: An Autobiography."

prised and converted the European music centers by his concerts in London, Paris, Berlin, in 1919-20. . . . As to Handy, it is well-known how between 1909 and 1912 he championed simon-pure and despised Mississippi folk music and finally in the latter year loosed the overwhelming flood of the Blues. . . . The leaders of this generation of Negro musicians had ideal goals and moral loyalties; theirs was not merely inborn musical talent and musical luck."

The Blues were not theatrical in their origin or in their spirit. Who first made them and out of what material, who sang them first and where and why, all these are questions answered variously and at great length by historians and writers on folk art. On one thing they all agree. True Blues are the individual's sorrow songs as the Spirituals are those of the group. A typical line is "I got the blues, an' too dam' mean to cry." What Isaac Goldberg said of ragtime might well be said of Blues: "They are in part the pagan release of the Negro from his addiction to holiness."

That the Blues have come to us so nearly in their pure folk-form is largely due to the fact that W. C. Handy's spirit was so much the spirit of the Blues that when he began writing in that form himself, and ever since, they have seemed to be his particular and personal creation. Handy was born in Florence, Alabama, in 1873. He was the son and grandson of Methodist ministers, and a career in music did not fit well into the family tradition. But even as a boy Handy could not resist the sound of Negro work songs or the quartets at the barber shops. He learned to play the cornet by ear, and, with that accomplishment as a starter, he traveled to the Chicago World's Fair where he joined a Negro minstrel troupe as bandleader. But soon he was home again, always and everywhere listening to the songs of Negro laborers, of sharecroppers, of the itinerant musicians who sang in Southern saloons or on the streets of Southern towns. And pretty soon he began to experiment in writing songs of his own in the Blues form.

The familiar rhythms and the basic tunes which Handy had collected during years of listening and research on Southern docks and rails, in factories and barrel-houses, were the materials on which he built. The "Memphis Blues" and the "St. Louis Blues," both very early, both in the true Blues form and spirit, are Handy's own, like scores of others. But the Blues have sprung, apparently spontaneously, from many places where Negroes lived and worked—from Beale Street, Memphis,

48

BESSIE SMITH, one of the early mastersingers of the Blues, who carries their stamp ineffacably traced on her features. With other famous singers like Ma Rainey, Clara and Mamie Smith she established the Blues in our musical pattern. Her phonograph records are collector's items.

49

from St. Louis cabarets, from the docks of New Orleans, from little, lonely towns all up and down the Mississippi. Today they are accepted as part of the nation's musical wealth. Their form has been appropriated; the newer lyrics are too often falsely sentimental, but when the Blues as a fashion have passed, the Blues as folk music will undoubtedly stay on. It is their source and their impact on the theatre that concerns us here. And at a time when so many types of Negro story are seen on the New York stage, it is significant of the double trend—to and away from folk literature—that a recent success (Countee Cullen's and Arna Bontemps' *St. Louis Woman*) should be based on one of the earliest and most famous of W. C. Handy's songs, the "St. Louis Blues":*

> I hate to see de evenin' sun go down
> I hate to see de evenin' sun go down
> Cause mah baby, he don lef' dis town.
>
> St. Louis woman wid her diamon' rings
> Pulls dat man aroun' by her apron strings.
> 'Twan't for powder an' for store-bought hair
> De man I love would not gone nowhere.
>
> Got de St. Louis blues, jes' as blue as I can be
> Dat man got a heart lak a rock cast in de sea
> Or else he wouldn't have gone so far from me

>   *   *   *   *   *

> Gypsy done tol' me, "Don't you wear no black."
> Yes, she done tol' me, "Don't you wear no black.
> Go to St. Louis, you can win him back."

>   *   *   *   *   *

> I loves dat man lak a schoolboy loves his pie
> Lak a Kentucky colonel loves his mint an' rye
> I'll love mah baby till de day I die.
>
> You ought to see dat stovepipe brown o' mine
> Lak he owns de Dimon' Joseph lines
> He'd make a cross-eyed 'oman go stone blind.
>
> Blacker than midnight, teeth lak flags of truce
> Blackest man in de whole St. Louis
> Blacker de berry, sweeter is de juice . . . .

50   *From "St. Louis Blues," by permission of the copyright owner, W. C. Handy.

The story of the Spirituals is both simpler and less simple than that of the Blues. It is clear that they are indeed "the siftings of centuries"; that they are the release, in song, of the Negro's religious fervor, his sorrows and his rebellion under slavery, his hope of a hereafter. What certain Spirituals have borrowed in phrase or melody from the folk songs of other races, or have taken over from church hymns, is only superficial. Even what memories of Africa they may carry seems of no great importance except to folklorists. They remain in their essence a characteristic expression of the musical genius of the American Negro. They are perhaps his greatest contribution to American musical literature. In their words, their harmonic style, in the Negro's way of singing them—which is the song—and especially in their choral singing, where they are at their best, the Spirituals are altogether and typically Negro. This is as true of songs like "Joshua Fit the Battle of Jericho" with its obvious Bible reflection, and of "Go Down Moses" with its refrain of "Set My People Free," as it is of the elemental and beautiful "I Know Moonrise!"

> I know moon-rise, I know star-rise,
>   I lay dis body down.
> I walk in de moonlight, I walk in de starlight,
>   To lay dis body down.
> I walk in de graveyard, I walk thru de graveyard,
>   To lay dis body down.
> I lie in de grave an' stretch out my arms,
>   I lay dis body down.
> I go to de jedgment in de evenin' of de day
>   When I lay dis body down,
> An' my soul an' your soul will meet in de day
>   When I lay dis body down.

It is almost three-quarters of a century ago that Fisk University, ambitious, young, desperately in need of funds, first sent out a specially trained chorus to sing Spirituals—then almost unknown except to Negroes—wherever an audience could be found to listen and to pay. The man who led them was George L. White, a blacksmith's son, born in a small New York village. He had fought through the Civil War and had served in the Freedman's Bureau at Nashville. On Sundays he taught a class of Negro children there, and, singing with them, came to know the Spirituals, or Jubilee Songs, as some of the Negroes called

THE SPIRITUALS or "Sorrow Songs" of the Negroes have been compared to the Psalms as an expression of deep religious emotion. All the finest Negro soloists feature them on their programs today but the true quality of the Spirituals is choral and is best expressed in group singing. Gjon Mili's camera pictures the excellent chorus of the Karamu Theatre in Cleveland singing "Goin' Down to the River."

them. From that day he felt that he had had a call to let the world hear those songs sung by Negroes. So he undertook to lead the pilgrimage of the Fisk Jubilee Singers—four boys and five girls—carrying with them for expenses, it is said, all of the scanty funds in the Fisk treasury except one dollar. They stopped at Wilberforce in Xenia, Ohio, oldest of Negro schools, where a Negro bishop gave them his blessing. Then they went on northward, meeting difficulty and discouragement always in the same way—with a song. Finally after a great burst of applause greeted the end of their concert at Oberlin, the world began to listen to them. Henry Ward Beecher invited them to come to Brooklyn and they made such an impression there that calls came pouring in from across the country and across the sea. They sang for seven years in England, Scotland, and Ireland, Holland, Switzerland and Germany. And, from their travels, they brought back $150,000 to Fisk University.

Other schools—Hampton, Tuskegee, Atlanta—soon had their Jubilee Choirs. But even more important, the songs—before this carried down by ear from one generation to the next—were collected, published and recorded.

It took a long time, however, before New York, either in the theatre or in the concert hall, actually appreciated the dramatic and emotional quality of the Spirituals and made them welcome. During the last quarter century, they have come down to us from many directions—from serious composers like Harry Burleigh and J. Rosamond Johnson, from singing orchestras like the Clef Club and the Hall Johnson Choir, and singers like Roland Hayes, Marian Anderson, Paul Robeson and Dorothy Maynor. Their popularity has mounted steadily. They have made effective the scenes in many plays. There is now hardly a day that goes by without Spirituals on the radio. They are constantly paid the doubtful compliment of imitation. Nor is it too much to say that the response of large audiences to the pure quality of this Negro folk music has stimulated the interest in other American folk songs—until recently living largely neglected in the hills and on the plains.

4

THE FOREGROUND: FROM 1917

W E SPEAK of the time after the beginning of the first World War as The Foreground, and date it from April, 1917, when the curtain went up on Ridgely Torrence's *Three Plays for a Negro Theatre*, at the Old Garden Theatre, formerly Wallack's, on the farther fringe of Broadway. The performance had what was probably the most nearly unanimous and spontaneous burst of critical approval a theatre performance in New York ever had—but more about that later. Actually, the rise of an earlier curtain should be noted as the beginning of The Foreground—the evening in March, 1914, when the Stage Society, urged on by Emilie Hapgood and Dorothy Donnelly, presented a double bill made up of Thomas Heywood's *A Woman Killed with Kindness* and Ridgely Torrence's Negro folk tragedy, *Granny Maumee*. Critics were either indifferent to Heywood's "quaint and gently pathetic Elizabethan relic" or disliked it heartily. But *Granny Maumee* attracted their keen interest as dramatic pioneering which deserved the heartiest encouragement. Nor was the author alone in finding favor. Torrence had intended the play for Negro actors, but Granny Maumee was a challenging role that suited Dorothy Donnelly's talents to perfection; she begged for the chance and had her way, to the play's advantage. Her playing was extraordinary both in its dignity and in its savage, eerie quality.

Granny Maumee is a Negro of royal African blood, proud of her

54

race, filled with hatred against the white men who had cost her her sight when she ventured too near the flames that burned her son for a murder he did not commit. When one of her granddaughters comes back to the cabin with a child tainted with white blood, Granny Maumee invokes ancient, magic curses upon the man who wrought her family this last unbearable injury. But she has lived too long in a Christian world; the spirit of forgiveness overcomes the voodoo and as Granny Maumee submits to its gentler power she dies.

That was a strong dose for a New York theatre audience, but the Stage Society rose to it with bravos. Almost immediately, Mr. Torrence's friends and the press united, loudly, in urging him to write more Negro plays. He did not, in fact, need such encouragement, for the idea had been in his mind a long time.

Mr. Torrence was already well known and highly regarded as a lyric poet, but his knowledge of stage techniques and of Negro life and character were unexpected. Yet the story of his life is its own explanation of this phase of his work. He was born and reared in Xenia, Ohio, a town which was, he says, more Southern than most Southern towns, although it was "just over the border." In the days before the Civil War, many plantation owners who no longer believed in slavery sold their slaves and their plantations and crossed over into Xenia. Sometimes the more energetic or the more dependent of their slaves would follow after them and there came to be, in Xenia, both a large, well-developed and prosperous Negro colony and a strong abolitionist group. Xenia became one of the most important "stations" on the slave "Underground Railway" and life was highly dramatic there. Generally speaking, the relations between the two races were friendly. Mr. Torrence remembers Negro boys in his class at high school, Negro members of the Presbyterian church to which he and his family belonged, and he still carries in his mind and heart the picture of the Negro hero of their sand-lot baseball team. The rhythm of Negro movement, the background and foreground of Negro history and religion, the music of Negro song and speech, were familiar to him from early childhood and made a special appeal to the poet within him. So when he started to write *Three Plays for a Negro Theatre,* the situations and the characters were already there in his mind and waiting to be released.

About this time the Irish dramatic revival, and especially the plays of Synge, filled the literary air. It has been assumed that Mr. Torrence was led to write his Negro plays under their influence. What actually happened was that as he read about the amateur players and the folk audience at the Abbey Theatre, he decided that Negro folk players and a folk audience—in a barn in his home town of Xenia, if necessary—were the solution for his own problem.

The Rider of Dreams, a Negro folk comedy, and *Simon the Cyrenian*, a "passion interlude" about the man who bore the cross for Jesus —with *Granny Maumee*—made up the *Three Plays for a Negro Theatre*. *Granny Maumee* is uneven in its texture, as if a weakness in the acting might easily harm it, but it has power and a strong climax. *Simon the Cyrenian*, more a religious pageant than a play, supplied a vivid contrast and, in Mrs. Hapgood's production, offered a fine opportunity to Inez Clough as Procula, the wife of Pontius Pilate. It was *The Rider of Dreams* that won the mind and the heart of every member of the audience. It tells the story of a pious, hard-working woman whose only ambition is to buy herself a little home. By long days of sacrifice she saves the necessary money. Her lazy husband, for whom life is chiefly song, steals the money from her, is robbed in turn, gets the money back and is completely happy because he can ride his dream again and make his own music. Nobody who saw Opal Cooper—and heard him as the dreamer, Madison Sparrow—will ever forget the lift his performance gave, the sound of his musical voice and the beauty of his measured movements as he recited the dream that he "dreamed right, face fo'mos' an' on de run.* . . . Las' night, an' day befo' yistiddy night, an' night befo' dat. I wuz layin' groanin', 'O Lawd, how long,' an' I heah a voice say, 'Git up an' come a-runnin'.' Looks up an' sees a fine w'ite saddle hoss. Hoss say,

" 'Ride me right an' I'll guide you right.'

"On I gits an' off he goes, slick as a rancid transom car. Come to high hill lookin' down on de sun an' moon. Hoss stop an' say,

'Brung you heah to give you noos
De worl' is youahn to pick an' choose.'
"I ax him 'How dat?' Hoss say:
'How is how an' why is why,
Buy low an' sell high.'
"I say to him, 'I got no money to buy. Wheah I goin' git de fun's to buy low?' Hoss respon':
'Trus' yo'se'f an' take youah own,
Git de meat an' leave de bone,

 *From *The Rider of Dreams*, in a book titled "Granny Maumee and Other Plays," by Ridgely Torrence. By permission of the Macmillan Co., Publishers, and of the author.

Bus' de nut an' fling em de shell,
Ride an' let em walk a spell,
Findeh's keepeh's, loseh's weepeh's,
I hope dese few lines find you well.'
"I ax him who tole him all dis an' hoss say:
'Ole hoss GRAB will nevah balk,
All dis heah is w'ite-man talk.'

"Dat what de hoss say to me in my true dream ev'y night dis week an' I'm a-goin' to bide by hit twell de las' er pea time. 'Cause I'm er true dreameh an' my mammy she wuz befo' me."

"It was not only the capacity of the Negro as an actor," Torrence said, "that I wished to exploit. It was also the extraordinary dramatic richness of his daily life. The Negro has been a race apart and usually a race in subjection. . . . Its life under slavery with its intense but seemingly hopeless longing for liberty produced in it a certain epic spirit, unconscious of course. . . . In modern life, the Negro comes face to face with many tragedies unknown to the Anglo-Saxon."

Mrs. Emilie Hapgood, who produced the plays, said quite simply that her object was to give a numerous and somewhat neglected race its first real chance in dramatic art. To give the plays the best possible opportunity, she engaged a young artist, who had already made a name as a scene designer, to set and costume the plays, and to direct them. It was Robert Edmond Jones' first professional assignment as director.

They gathered together their cast after long and serious search in half a dozen cities, and the players, many of whom were familiar names at the Lafayette, met their challenge so well that the critical fraternity were taken off their feet.

By a happy chance there has recently come to hand a book of press clippings made by a man who was interested in preserving, for his personal use, the record of the extraordinary response to these plays.

Robert Benchley saw a dress rehearsal and wrote of it in the "Tribune":

"In the Negro, there is a natural beauty of voice, a musical sense of rhythm, a plasticity of pose and emotional richness which can not be equalled in any other race. It is on these qualities that Mr. Torrence has tried to make his *Three Plays* depend. . . . There will be no Negro minstrelsy and no tawdry imitation of white folks' melodrama. . . . I saw one lithe youth who was rehearsing the part of an Egyptian slave

57

A DRAWING of Simon the Cyrenian made by Djuna Barnes to accompany her review of Ridgely Torrence's *Three Plays for a Negro Theatre.*

make an obeisance before the King (who was not there). It was a move which, if it were being rehearsed by an average actor, would have to be done over 25 times and then probably abandoned as impossible. At the first time this boy, out of his own intuitive sense of what was right, made as perfect and complete a gesture as could have been drawn with a pair of compasses and with infinitely more animation. Mr. Torrence has a large vision. He hopes that these plays will serve as a foundation for a movement that will eventually need an organization of its own to carry it on. . . . It all depends on the spirit in which the public receives them. If they go expecting to see burlesque, they will not only be disappointed; they will be ashamed."

Francis Hackett wrote in "The New Republic": "It is, all things considered, as fine an enterprise as the American theatre has seen for years. One undiscovered country in emotional America is Negro country and these productions have disclosed it in a fresh and vigorous and lovely way. . . . The actors had unusual power and charm."

Frank Crane wrote in the "Globe," "If a highly cultured and entirely unprejudiced foreigner were to look for the most interesting theatre in the city, he would find it here. These Negroes play Negro plays. They reveal the soul of the people. They are not propagandizing. They do not demand, argue, or protest. They are really artists."

Negro critics joined heartily in the praise.

James Weldon Johnson in "The New York Age" said: "We do not know how many colored people of greater New York realize that April, 1917, marks an epoch for the Negro on the stage. Mrs. Emilie Hapgood has given the American Negro his first opportunity in serious legitimate drama. It is amazing how Mr. Torrence, a white man, could write plays of Negro life with such intimate knowledge, with such deep insight and sympathy."

The *Three Plays* opened on April 5, 1917. On April 6, America declared war. Randolph Bourne, that sensitive artist and penetrating critic whose early death was a major loss to American literature, was at the Garden Theatre that day and he wrote about it:

". . . It was Good Friday. And it was the day of the proclamation of war. As the solemn tones pealed out in the last play *Simon, the Cyrenian*, with its setting for the Crucifixion—'They that take the sword shall perish by the sword'—you could hear the audience catch its breath as it realized the piercing meaning of this heroic little drama of non-resistance played before a Christian nation that was going into a world war on the very day that its churches celebrated devoutly the anniversary of this very warning. . . . It seems imperative that no person with imagination miss this genuine dramatic experience."

Added to the lure of the plays and the acting was another new feature—the entr'acte music—a singing orchestra of Clef Club members, led by J. Rosamond Johnson. They played folk music and sang Spirituals, songs still largely fresh and new in a white theatre world. Few people left their seats between the acts.

Yet within a few weeks this brilliant venture had ended. The impact of the war on the whole theatre was too strong to withstand. Mrs. Hapgood moved her company up to the Garrick, nearer the theatre audience, but that did not help much. The first fine emotion was gone.

There has been more space given to *Three Plays for a Negro Theatre* in this record than will be given to anything else. Not because the plays themselves were as important dramatically as a great many things that came later, but for other reasons. They marked, it was agreed, a turning point in Negro theatre history. They broke completely with all the theatre stereotypes of Negro character. They gave Negro actors a first fine opportunity. They made Negroes welcome in the audience. They showed that Negroes could appreciate a white man's contribution to the literature of their life, if it were written in truth and beauty. They showed how a healthy criticism responds to a healthy stimulus. Above all, they showed that the *Three Plays* were not a happy accident. They were the distillation of a lyric poet's long thinking and experience of life; they were the end product of faithful training by certain actors and musicians. All of this, plus the considered intention of a producer with courage and imagination and a designer-director of unusual talent. Such things do not, in the theatre, "just happen"; but they *can* happen at any time when men and the stars will it so.

5

BRIGHT LIGHTS ON BROADWAY 1920

Iᴛ ᴡᴀs three years later that Eugene O'Neill burst into swift and lasting fame with *The Emperor Jones*, produced at the Provincetown Playhouse with Charles Gilpin as the Emperor. The tiny theatre on MacDougal Street, with its new talents, fresh faces and new forms, had already found a favoring audience for plays by new playwrights. O'Neill himself had attracted attention with several of his sea plays. He had already shown himself to be a master of theatre speech and to know how to round out the characters of the typical men and women whom he had met in his wandering life. Add to these O'Neill's gift for fantasy and the spirit is clear in which he started to search out exactly the right player for the fascinating role of the pullman porter turned Emperor of a jungle island. He found him in Harlem, where Charles Gilpin was no stranger to theatre folk. He had played in the Williams and Walker shows, in the Pekin stock company in Chicago, with the Lafayette Players. He had been noticed recently for an excellent portrayal of the Reverend William Custis in John Drinkwater's *Abraham Lincoln*. But there was not always theatre work for a Negro actor of his power and sometimes he worked for a printer or ran an elevator between theatre jobs. He was doing something of the kind when the Provincetown Players found him. He had just the talents needed to portray the protagonist of O'Neill's play, the man half-primitive and half-bluff, pursued by fate and human enmity and even more by his

61

CHARLES GILPIN, as the Emperor Jones, shared the great success of that play with Eugene O'Neill and also received a citation for one of the season's best pieces of acting. It did not, however, save him from the necessity of earning his living by running an elevator again when *The Emperor Jones* ended. In a recent interview Eugene O'Neill is quoted as saying that Charles Gilpin was the only actor he remembered who had done exactly what he intended in a role, neither more nor less.

own fear of a silver bullet that should cause his death. As soon as the play and the player met they became one, and although *The Emperor Jones* has gone around the world, and has been made into a motion picture, made into an opera, and played before the television camera, the portrait of the Emperor is still recognized as Gilpin's contribution to the American theatre almost as much as it is O'Neill's.

The drama played to crowded houses downtown and later uptown throughout many months. Gilpin's performance was named one of the ten best in the New York theatre that year. But when the long run of the play was over, Gilpin was soon running an elevator again.

There was one man who saw more clearly than most what Gilpin's performance and its public response meant. Bert Williams was already a sick man in 1920. For twenty years he had hoped for a part of that stature. But he watched Gilpin with pride and pleasure unmixed with envy. He foresaw what Gilpin's success in this spectacular major role would do for the Negro in the American theatre. It was too late for Williams, almost too late for Gilpin, but it was a long step forward.

The next important entry was a very special case, much easier to deal with than the *Three Plays* and *The Emperor Jones*. *Shuffle Along* asked only to be enjoyed. It was a revue, acted and produced by Negroes, written by Negroes for Negro audiences. An accumulation of talent was its chief producing capital; in fact, was almost all the capital it had. The company, organized in New York, had an opportunity to open at the Howard Theatre in Washington, but they did not even have money enough to pay their railroad fares. After a good deal of effort, they leaped that hurdle, played two weeks to good houses and saved enough to go on to another Negro theatre, the Dunbar in Philadelphia. Two standing-room-only weeks there brought the company intact, but breathless, into the old and unkempt 63rd St. Theatre in New York. Almost before it had settled down there, *Shuffle Along* was a smash hit. It played New York for over a year and wandered around the country for two years more. Everybody was singing its hit songs, "I'm Just Wild About Harry," "Love Will Find a Way," "Bandana Days," and, after the record was established, everyone wondered why anyone should have doubted the popularity of a show that had Sissle and Blake at its musical helm, Miller and Lyles as chief comedians, and Florence Mills in her first important role.

When *Shuffle Along* was first conceived, it was probably thought

63

MILLER AND LYLES had found and held a large and eager audience in vaudeville long before Broadway succumbed to them in *Shuffle Along*, *Runnin' Wild* and *Rang-Tang*. They were expert comedians and, unlike most teams, they had not one but a whole series of first-rate acts on which they improvised freely.

NOBLE SISSLE AND EUBIE BLAKE have worked separately or together in many shows and in many capacities. Mr. Sissle succeeded Jim Europe as bandmaster of the 15th Regiment in World War I. With Blake (seated here at the piano) he composed and conducted *Shuffle Along*. They wrote *The Chocolate Dandies,* which had Inez Clough as leading lady, Johnny Hudgins, a top-flight dancing comedian, and Josephine Baker. Together they wrote several popular World War II camp shows.

65

of entirely in terms of Negro entertainment. It was Harlem, but with a folk angle. It did not bother to make concessions to white taste or to theatre clichés. It was a good, honest, fast-moving, sometimes sentimental, sometimes satirical, funny and melodious show. And there has never been anything else quite like it.

The Negroes had half-a-dozen outstanding examples of the two-man teams popular for so many years in vaudeville and revues. Sometimes these teams were two comedians, sometimes two singing actors or dancing actors or a dancer and a musical performer of one kind or another, or two composer-performers. Sometimes many of these talents were combined in a single team. Miller and Lyles were remarkable for the fact that they were two expert comedians neither of whom played the other into the shadow. They had "packed them in" in vaudeville and in Harlem long before they came to Broadway. Many teams (both black and white) had only one first-rate act which they used with slight variants for years. Miller and Lyles had any number and improvised freely on all of them. Before Aubrey Lyles died in 1933, they wrote the scripts of several shows, including *Runnin' Wild*. *Runnin' Wild* did not have quite as steady a pulse as *Shuffle Along,* but the name song, by A. Harrington Gibbs, was outstanding and the whole show was good, good enough to run eight months and to introduce the Charleston, with the music of James Johnson, to American dance floors.

Noble Sissle and Eubie Blake appeared in *Shuffle Along* not only as composers but as conductor and performer, Sissle with his "take it from me" kind of singing and Blake at the piano, both wholly satisfying and expert. And like all Negro composers they were assured in advance that the bands who played their music would know how jazz should sound and that their dancers would have "the essential feelings for rhythm and broken rhythm in their bones." Sissle and Blake wrote *The Chocolate Dandies* in 1924. It had an excellent cast including Inez Clough and Johnny Hudgins, a top-flight dancing comedian. Then Sissle went to London; Blake wrote the score for *The Blackbirds of 1929*. Ever since then, Sissle and Blake have been among Negro leaders in the entertainment field and have contributed to the success of many musical comedies and night club shows. Sissle followed Jim Europe as bandmaster of the 15th Regiment in World War I. His band was for many years among the most famous of the name bands. And, to bring their record down to date, Sissle was on the board of Camp Shows, Inc., in World War II

66

Edward Steichen: from the February 1925 Vanity Fair © The Condé Nast Pubs.

FLORENCE MILLS, who never failed to find the straightest road to the heart of any audience, with her singing and her dancing, in *Dixie to Broadway.*

and he and Blake worked together again writing lively shows for USO, including *Harlem on Parade* and *The Sepia and Swing Revolution*.

And so to Florence Mills, of whom Gilbert Seldes wrote in "The Seven Lively Arts": *

". . . merely to watch her walk out upon the stage with her long, free stride and her superb, shameless swing, is an aesthetic pleasure; she is a school and exemplar of carriage and deportment; two other actors I have seen so take a stage; Cohan by stage instinct, Marie Tempest by a cultivated genius. Florence Mills is almost the definition of the romantic *une force qui va,* but she remains an original, with little or nothing to give beyond her presence, her instinctive grace, and her baffling, seductive voice."

Since there was no doubt that she had a delightful presence, a natural charm, projection, grace, and the voice of a bird turned woman, what, one might well ask, did this alluring little dancer lack? She did not have Lily Pons' high notes or Bert Williams' comic humor or Marian Anderson's technique, but what she had was enough to keep an audience's eyes glued to her every moment of her performance, to keep an ear fascinated by the music and color of her voice. When she sang and danced at the Palace, you would have to go early to find a seat, and in the audience you would see artists with their sketch books, dancers, poets, whom you gradually came to know as among Florence Mills' most admiring fans.

Her part in *Shuffle Along* was her first major role and she came to that by accident through the illness of Gertrude Saunders, a popular Negro comedienne. Florence Mills' early years were pretty much like Gertrude Lawrence's, except that she was "discovered" as a child prodigy and that the poor vaudeville companies she travelled with during her early days were perhaps a shade poorer than those Lawrence knew. It was a big day for Florence Mills when she played in the second company of *The Sons of Ham* as a singer and dancer. Like Opal Cooper, she came to Broadway from a Harlem night club. And then, almost at once, everything good came to her. The critics all liked her; the audience adored her. She could have had almost anything she wanted in her field. *Shuffle Along* played for a year and then she went as a star into Lew Leslie's *Plantation Revue*, first at a night club, then enlarged at the 48th St. Theatre. The next year, Lew Leslie took her to London. The English critics responded to her as they did to Williams and Walker. Even

 *From "The Seven Lively Arts," by Gilbert Seldes. By permission of the author, and of the publishers, Harper and Brothers.

such a highbrow as St. John Ervine said: "The success acquired by Miss Florence Mills, the American colored girl, playing in *From Dover to Dixie,* is something unequalled by any American playing here in the past decade. She is by far the most artistic person London has had the good fortune to see." Later, Leslie brought her to New York with much the same script, which he called *Dixie to Broadway.*

In 1926, she went back to Harlem in a show written specially for her, and made to her measure, called *Blackbirds.* After six weeks at the Alhambra Theatre, Lew Leslie again crossed the ocean with his company, taking it boldly to Paris where it ran for six months. From there it went to London, where, according to press reports, the Prince of Wales saw it sixteen times. The little star and her Blackbirds came back in high fettle and found a New York audience waiting eagerly for her, waiting to hear her favorite song "I'm a Little Blackbird Looking for a Bluebird." But again, as so often with talented Negro players, with Bob Cole, George Walker, Bert Williams, death came too early. A delayed operation for appendicitis cost this lovely creature her life before *Blackbirds* could open. All of New York sorrowed; all of Harlem wept. "We have so few," they said, "She was so young."

The Dance and Some Dancers: An Interlude

It took a good deal of courage for Lew Leslie to bring the *Blackbirds* of 1928 to the stage without Florence Mills. But he had the makings of a good show and another Negro musical had met with some success during the season: *Rang-Tang,* with Miller and Lyles, Daniel Haynes, Evelyn Preer. It looked as if Leslie could make a go of it if he could add to his company (that already included Adelaide Hall, Ada Ward, Johnny Hudgins) a man strong enough to hold the show together. He knew a man who was a genius in his own particular form of dance and who, he thought, might be counted upon to carry the load—if he could be lured away from big-time vaudeville, where his audience was secure. His name was Bill Robinson. Harlem called him Bojangles; they also called him the best tap dancer in the world, and Harlem was right. *Blackbirds* was a lively show with several hit songs—"Diga Diga Do," "I Can't Give You Anything But Love," "I Must Have That Man"— and, for over 500 performances, Bill Robinson and a first-class band and ensemble danced it to success.

Bill Robinson has danced many a show to success since *Blackbirds*—

in productions like *Brown Buddies,* in popular night club shows, and even in the movies where he taught Shirley Temple the mysteries of the tap. When we can stop enjoying Bill Robinson long enough to think about what he is doing and with what skill he does it, we can come closer than anywhere else, perhaps, to understanding the essential quality that has made for the success of Negroes in the complex pattern of the theatre: namely, the intimate relationship between the arts that they seem to accept instinctively. André Levinson, Europe's most distinguished critic of the dance, showed his usual insight when he recognized the fact, twenty years ago, that the drummer who is the soul of any jazz band is essentially a dancer.

The dance has everywhere been the cradle of music and to the Negro —actor, dancer, singer, musician—dance *is* music; music is action, is joy and sorrow, love and prayer, and the artist and his audience are expected to move as one. What is true of the Negro preacher and his swaying congregation, of the jazz-band leader and his cavorting men is also true of the actor-dancer and his responsive audience.

Mary Austin, who understood the American rhythm so well, gave her testimony to this in writing about Bill Robinson just after he developed that marvelous tap dance up and down a stair that electrified every audience that saw—and heard—it, and danced with it, within themselves. "It is safe to say that Bill Robinson's audience," she wrote, "knows no more than Bill of what . . . is going on before its eyes. It probably does not realize in any formal way that he is offering them the great desideratum of modern art, a clean short cut to areas of enjoyment long closed to us by the accumulated rubbish of the culture route. For Bill Robinson not only restores to us our primal rhythmic appreciations; he himself reaches the sources of his rhythmic inspiration by paths that the modern American artist would give one of his eyes—the eye filmed and colored by five thousand years of absorbed culture—to feel beneath his feet. . . . In such release and return lies the chief gift of the Negro to contemporary art. . . ."

There have been at least a score of other Negro dancers *almost* as good as Bill Robinson (and many of them his pupils) since he pointed the way. Some of them—from Johnny Hudgins to Avon Long—have had a comedian's or a singer's talent in addition to their dancing. There have been jolly teams like the Nicholas Brothers, recently enlivening *St. Louis Woman,* and lately a dancer and choreographer of unusual talent,

70

BILL ROBINSON, affectionately known as "Bojangles," a tap dancer without peer.

KATHERINE DUNHAM with Archie Savage and Talley Beatty in "Ti' Cocomacaque." Miss Dunham is an anthropologist. But since she believes that the forms and traditions of the dance are among the most permanent of a race's cultural links with the past she has done much of her scientific delving in that field. Then, as dancer and choreographer, she has recreated some of the native themes into theatre terms. Beginning with a small but talented group in a recital of Caribbean folk dances she grew to full proportions in the 1947 *Bal Negre*.

Pearl Primus, a soloist in the revival of *Showboat*. But it has remained for a young Negro woman dancer actually to go back and search out the sources of Negro dance that interested Mary Austin and André Levinson so deeply.

Katherine Dunham, born in Chicago in 1912, is a dancer and an anthropologist. Forms of the dance, she believes, have greater tenacity than any other cultural forms and as such are part of the anthropologist's essential material. She undertook to offer evidence of this when the Rosenwald Foundation awarded her a fellowship to study native dancing in Jamaica, Martinique, Trinidad and Haiti. The rich notes she brought back from these tours were interpreted in illuminating articles, as guest choreographer with the Chicago Federal Theatre, and vividly in later series of concerts (presented with her group) illustrating authentic native dances of the United States and the Caribbean. These were followed by dances in the musical, *Cabin in the Sky*, where her playing as the Scarlet Woman showed her to be not only an admirable dancer with magnificent rhythm and a wide range of dance-expression, but a singer who could put over a song—like "There's Honey in the Honeycomb."

Another Negro dancer, famous a little earlier, was almost the antithesis of Katherine Dunham. She had probably been singing and dancing in choruses for some time before she first attracted notice in Sissle and Blake's *Chocolate Dandies*. Every time the lively dance chorus in that show appeared, some quite inexplicable attraction drew the eyes of the audience to a little girl with flaming eyes, a body that was the epitome of dance, and an unbeautiful, but fascinating, trick of pushing her head forward on her little neck as some young animal might when he scented food ahead. Before many weeks had gone by, Josephine Baker's name was appearing frequently in print. It was obvious that no chorus would hold her long. But few people anticipated her fiery history that belongs to the record of the Negro theatre in America chiefly because its sources and its impulses were there.

Josephine Baker was not an artist in the sense that Florence Mills was. She was a "natural," with an uncanny power of projecting her personality and her talent. After several flashes in New York, she went to Paris with the *Revue Nègre* and stayed there for many years achieving a strange theatrical and personal fame and a fortune. André Levinson gave serious attention to her dancing. He called Baker "a sinuous idol

73

that enslaves and incites mankind. Thanks to her carnal magnificence," he wrote, "her exhibition comes close to pathos. It was she who led the spellbound drummer and the fascinated saxophonist in the harsh rhythm of the Blues. It was as though the jazz, catching on the wing the vibrations of this mad body, were interpreting, word by word, its fantastic monologue. The music is born from the dance and what a dance! Certain of Miss Baker's poses . . . had the compelling potency of the finest examples of Negro sculpture. It was no longer a grotesque dancing girl that stood before the audience, but the Black Venus that haunted Baudelaire." Of herself and her dancing, Josephine Baker had this to say: *"Pourquoi je suis devenue danseuse? Parce que je suis née dans une ville froide* [St. Louis], *parce que j'ai eu très froid durant toute mon enfance. J'ai eu froid et j'ai dansé pour avoir chaud."*

When she returned to New York some years later in a show called *At Home Abroad,* her talents were warped and her power was already on the wane. But there must have been something of the original flame still burning, for Lt. Morton Eustis wrote from a front-line camp in North Africa: "You might be interested to hear about the double-feature show we had at camp last night, one starring Josephine Baker in person. . . .

"A sergeant M.C. started off the show by introducing the orchestra and giving the audience a brief program note on Josephine Baker's background. . . .

"Then Miss Baker, in a flamboyant costume of vertical purple and red stripes, with a flowing skirt and puffed sleeves, swept onto the stage and up to the mike. She looked the audience over, smiled mischievously, gave an impudent wiggle . . . then, as a gasp of pleasure rippled through the audience, she stood delightedly waving at 'the boys.' The 'boys,' needless to say, roared their approval.

"Her first number was an American ditty as sly and insinuating as the curves, bumps and contortions of the dusky 'Vedette' herself, 'La Grande Vedette Americaine,' as she was billed in the heyday of her fame in Paris. I remember seeing her at the Casino de Paris with Maurice Chevalier—before the crash of '29—the toast of the fashionable world.

"Here she was years later, on a platform in one corner of a dusty field in Africa—no older apparently, no less dexterous in putting over a song, in punctuating every line with an appropriate twist of her body —standing them up in the aisles (literally and to roars of disapproval

74

from the soldiers seated in the rear) and holding the audience with as much ease as if both she and they had all the facilities of a comfortable theatre at their disposal. . . . Her evident enjoyment of the furore she was creating was as infectious as the lilt of her strident voice and the brazen strut with which she sidled about the stage."

JOSEPHINE BAKER *in a French revue, at the height of her European popularity.*

6

PLAYS AND PLAYERS

Music and dance were not going their way alone in the 20's and 30's. Far from it! These were the most rewarding, as well as the most glamorous, days in all American theatre history. The Neighborhood Playhouse, under the guidance of Alice and Irene Lewisohn, The Provincetown Playhouse, The Theatre Guild, and Arthur Hopkins were flourishing. A group of young artists—Robert Edmond Jones, Lee Simonson, Norman Geddes, Aline Bernstein, James Reynolds—brought not only their skill as designers, but their creative interest in all theatre arts. Eugene O'Neill, Maxwell Anderson, Elmer Rice, Paul Green, Robert Sherwood were directing the currents of playwriting into new and broader channels. John Barrymore, Walter Huston, Katharine Cornell, Helen Hayes, the Lunts were reaching new heights in acting. America welcomed visitors like the Abbey Theatre, Max Reinhardt and the Moscow Art Theatre. Running side by side with all this, there was an earnest attempt to re-awaken Negro interest in serious plays of every kind and to re-establish a Negro theatre. Eugene O'Neill's *Dreamy Kid*, produced at the Provincetown, dealt forthrightly with Negro superstition and gangster life. Paul Green's charming fantasy *The No 'Count Boy* was brought to New York by the Carolina Playmakers and carried off the award in the Little Theatre Tournament, bringing to national attention a playwright the best of whose talents have been devoted to plays of Negro life.

Frank Wilson, already known as a versatile Negro actor, had his first showing as a dramatist with *Sugar Cane. Strut, Miss Lizzie,* by Creamer and Layton, opened in Chicago and soon had everyone singing "Sweet Angelina." Ernest Culbertson with *Goat Alley,* Nan Bagby Stephens with *Roseanne* attracted attention and favorable notices for realistic dramas. Mary Hoyt Wiborg wrote an African voodoo play, *Taboo,* more notable for its players than for its drama, since Paul Robeson made his first appearance professionally as the voodoo King to Margaret Wycherly's voodoo Queen.

From Chicago, Raymond O'Neil and Mrs. Sherwood Anderson brought the Ethiopian Art Players to Harlem. They tried a repertory that included well-known modern plays, dramas of Negro life and classics. Harlem was not as kind to them as it should have been, considering the talent the Players represented, so the producers bravely brought their company to Broadway to try their luck. One program, at least, had its due reward. It was made up of *The Chipwoman's Fortune,* the first serious play by a Negro author, Willis Richardson, that was well received; and *Salome* with Evelyn Preer, on which several of the critics, including George Jean Nathan, reported very favorably.

Another production, which has been more noted in retrospect than it was at the time, was a version of *The Comedy of Errors.* The scene was a circus tent, the music was jazz—already thoroughly at home in the dance halls and no longer a stranger to the concert stage. It was not, however, until almost fifteen years later, in the days of the Federal Theatre, that swinging the classics became the fashion. In the 1920's, audiences did not like to see Shakespeare intruded upon. The Ethiopian Art Players disbanded.

In the meantime Eugene O'Neill had taken center stage again; this time with a full-length play that involved many of the problems on which the newer Negro drama has centered. It was a clear indication that an end had come to the era when the Negro's contribution to the theatre was limited to the comedian, the dancer, the composer, the popular singer. The actor and the material of drama were to the fore.

The Provincetown Players announced a production (1924) of *All God's Chillun Got Wings* with Paul Robeson playing the leading role, and the storm broke. In fact the thunder did not wait for the production of the play. Several months earlier the "American Mercury" published the script. It told the story of a young Negro intellectual who marries a white woman and with her fights an unrelenting fight against racial antagonism. Almost immediately, the yellow journals started a campaign against the production, employing every means within their power to stop it. News stories, headlines, and editorials were used to stimulate public disapproval and even to secure police protection against the performance. There was plenty of sound and plenty of fury. But the Provincetown Players stood their ground and their audience stood with them.

The night that the play opened the house was full. Both audience and actors were tense, fully expecting some outside interference; but nothing happened. The play ran smoothly. It was too bad that it was not a better and more convincing play. Negroes did not like it because, as one critic said, O'Neill "made the white girl who was willing to marry the black student, and whom he is glad to get, about as lost as he could well make her." Critics in general did not like it because O'Neill ripped the foundation away from the theme of the drama when he permitted the girl—weak by nature—to go mad under the strain of public prejudice. This changed the emphasis at once from the problem of whether happiness could be achieved in our present society by racial intermarriage, to the problem of how an intelligent man, already under social pressure, could live with a wife who was insane, however much he loved her. The play, in spite of this fundamental weakness, was boldly written and excellently played by both Robeson and Mary Blair. Robeson immediately became an actor to be reckoned with and when the play was soon followed (also at the Provincetown) by his first concert of Spirituals and Negro work songs, his reputation was established.

As we look back upon *All God's Chillun Got Wings* after twenty years, it is clear that its importance lay chiefly in its repercussions, in the critical analysis of the drama and the acting that it stimulated. Practically every question relating to the future of the Negro in the American theatre came to the surface there: Is the Negro actor an artist or is he, when he is good, only "a natural?" What is Negro drama? Has Negro life anything of importance to contribute to the main stream of American drama? Or is the drama of Negro life a separate thing, insofar as it exists at all? If it has something to contribute, what is its range? Do Negroes understand how to write about Negroes better than white men do, or vice versa? Are Negroes capable of enough technical discipline to write well for the theatre? All of these questions, the discussion about *All God's Chillun Got Wings* pointed up in newspapers, magazines and books. Many of them the plays of the last twenty years have outmoded. For more of them the years have at least suggested the answers.

Negro actors like Richard Harrison, Frank Wilson, Rose McClendon gave answer to the first question; but, by a strange quirk, Paul Robeson's relation to acting as an art still remained for a long time partly unanswered, even to himself. He has a majestic theatre presence, a power of projection that is as clear and sure in his acting as in his singing, a fine voice, a deep human understanding and sympathy that can measure any role he undertakes. Yet his next excursion into the theatre, *Black Boy*, by Jim Tully and Frank Dazey, a story of a Negro prizefighter, added nothing to his stature. And, as he himself says, until Othello came his way it never seemed worth all the labor it took to plumb the technical details of a role as it did to seek out the last nuance of a song.

As a general rule there is no remark that is so disparaging to the Negro actor, singer, musician, as the one—often intended as a high compliment—that he is a natural born actor, who does not benefit by training. It is true that the Negro often carries with him, as gifts of race or environment, an unfettered rhythmic sense, both in movement and speech, and a voice of more than ordinary range and flexibility. The impulse to dance and to sing as a group is strong both in his religious and his social traditions. So Negroes seem to fall naturally into an acted group scene, giving a sense of the whole and yet retaining an individual characterization, as Russian actors have been trained so admirably to do. Negro group dances are notable for their unity of line and freedom of rhythm, much of which has probably come down from tribal days and been nurtured in performance, as in the Saturday night dances in Congo Square in New Orleans, which Ridgely Torrence celebrated in his ballet pantomime, *Dance Calinda*. But all of these natural and traditional gifts are only first stepping stones to acting. Peasants of certain other races —the Hungarians, the Czechs, and the peasant Ukrainians—show much the same talents, though perhaps not to the same degree. But rhythm, no matter how beautiful, is not art. The winds have it and the waves and birds in flight. It is the mastery of rhythm, its discipline in acting, singing and dancing that serves the processes of art. The very overflow of rhythm characteristic of the Negro is what makes it so difficult for any but an experienced and sure-handed director to handle him on the stage. Anyone who has watched the rehearsal of a second-rate Negro company or seen a performance by untrained or badly directed Negro actors, has no difficulty in marking the stretch between natural gifts and disciplined talents. It is due to the versatility and skill of players who were sternly bred under Bob Cole's direction, or Bert Williams', or J. Leubrie Hill's, or later under James Light, Rouben Mamoulian, John Houseman, that today a role that calls for a Negro, no matter how demanding, is always played by a Negro.

It was almost two years after *All God's Chillun Got Wings* that the Provincetown Playhouse was again the scene of an important play of Negro life, Paul Green's *In Abraham's Bosom*. Mr. Green had already written many short plays of Negro life, both gay and sad, and had learned much from seeing them on the stage of The Carolina Playmakers. But this was his first full-length play professionally produced. Either by nature or by long association with Negroes at their homely task of pulling a living out of Carolina soil, he has a sense of speech-rhythm almost as free as theirs. The roles in *In Abraham's Bosom*, difficult though they were, were such as Negro actors of training and experience could appreciate and respond to. The three leading players in *In Abraham's Bosom* were Jules Bledsoe (shortly succeeded by Frank Wilson) as Abraham McCranie, Rose McClendon as his wife, Abbie Mitchell as her mother. It is difficult to remember scenes in any play that were more compelling than the tragic scenes in which these three players appeared together— all artists, all with long theatre training, all understanding that unity among players which the Russians call "communion." *In Abraham's Bosom* tells the story of a young Negro farmer who loses his life in a vain effort to find it for himself and for his people through education. His own people are hostile to his ideas; most of his white neighbors are openly antagonistic. Poverty and tragedy stalk his home and finally, in a mad moment, he kills his white half-brother and is lynched. It is a ruthless play, true in its essence, and deeply moving. It was accorded the Pulitzer Prize for 1926 and the actors shared the honors with the playwright.

In the same year in which *In Abraham's Bosom* was produced, David Belasco mounted *Lulu Belle*, by Charles MacArthur and Edward Sheldon, with all the trimmings that he knew so well how to provide. *Lulu Belle* was superficial but skilfully theatrical, and it attained an added success largely due to good acting and to a growing curiosity about street and

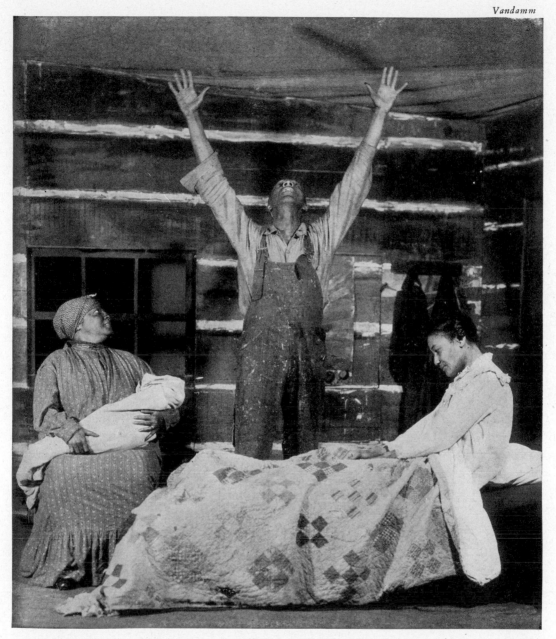

IN ABRAHAM'S BOSOM, the 1926 Pulitzer Prize Play by Paul Green, with the actors who shared the playwright's laurels: Frank Wilson as Abraham McCranie, Rose McClendon as his wife, Abbie Mitchell as her mother.

LULU BELLE, by Edward Sheldon and Charles MacArthur, was a lurid melodrama of Harlem life that offered David Belasco just the kind of realistic opportunity he enjoyed—great crowds, vivid contrasts, rapid action. For *Lulu Belle* he picked a mixed group of Negro and white actors, headed by Lenore Ulric, Henry Hull and Evelyn Preer (later succeeded by Edna Thomas). There was a good deal of romance rose-lighting the drama's realism, and there was no doubt of its success with audiences. There is little doubt that it hastened the presentation of other plays of Negro life, especially those with Harlem as a background.

underworld life in Harlem. Lenore Ulric played a Negro harlot, the central figure; Henry Hull the Negro barber; and both parts were remarkable for fidelity to type. There was a large cast, half of it Negro, to point up Belasco's realistic touches. Evelyn Preer (succeeded by Edna Thomas) carried off with success the role of Ruby Lee, second only to that of Miss Ulric. The settings of the play: Act I, a street scene in the San Juan Hill district; II, the top floor of a Harlem boarding house; III, a Harlem cabaret; IV, five years later, a luxurious apartment in Paris. Harlem was the play's real protagonist as it was to be in many plays in the years to come.

For by this time Harlem had become a city within a city. It held more Negroes than any other community anywhere, and more kinds of Negroes. There are said to be 50,000 West Indian Negroes in Harlem; a settled Portuguese colony, a considerable group of native Africans, speaking several different tongues; a small body of Abyssinian Jews. Southern Negroes coming North by the thousands, looking for jobs or for the younger, more adventurous, members of their family who have gone before, head straight for Harlem. Southern preachers follow their migrating congregations to Harlem and establish new cults there to battle for place and for funds with almost every known form of religious worship. Night life in Harlem, with music and dance and food and drink, is almost as active as life by day. Harlem is a place of crowded streets and overcrowded houses, the home of the numbers racket and policy kings, of strutters and gangsters and rabble-rousers. There is material for character comedy, for race protest and melodrama in Harlem.

It happens, however, that Harlem, besides being the center of all this intensely theatrical life, is also the home of a far larger community of Negroes—professional men of every kind, business men, artists, actors, musicians, tradesmen, white collar workers—who live and labor as quietly and earnestly, as hopefully and thoughtfully, as sociably and lonesomely, as all kinds and conditions of men do elsewhere in this great network of individuals and families and peoples that we call New York. But the trouble with this Harlem, as far as its contribution to play material is concerned, is that its comedy and its conflicts are too often too much like those of everybody else to make a separate, dramatic strand. They could just as easily be transposed to Park Avenue or Greenwich Village or Brooklyn.

All of which makes it seem likely that plays about Negroes in Harlem, if they are to be interesting and distinctive (and whether or not they are written by Negroes) will probably go on being folk plays or character comedies or melodramas or plays of race protest until they are secure enough to be just plays about people who happen to be Negroes.

*   *   *   *   *

After which tour around Harlem, induced by the audience's reaction to *Lulu Belle,* we come back once more to Broadway to hear Burns Mantle sum up the season 1927-28 in "The Best Plays": "It was nothing much to brag of as seasons go, nor one of which we were exactly ashamed. As we say of the comedy that doesn't quite come off, 'it was fairly stupid but it had its points.' "

There were 270 productions that season including forty revivals. Of these only something more than thirty were moderately successful. But among that 30 were *Strange Interlude, Marco Millions, The Royal Family, Coquette, The Letter, Paris Bound, The Queen's Husband, Volpone, Diamond Lil* and *Porgy.* It seems remarkable enough that Mr. Mantle should call a season mediocre that had so many outstanding plays. But it is even more remarkable that almost twenty years later so many of the most successful plays should seem farther away and more dated than *Porgy,* Du Bose and Dorothy Heyward's dramatization of Mr. Heyward's novel.

Porgy was produced by the Theatre Guild with Rouben Mamoulian directing. It was the story—panoramic, melodramatic, sordid, but both human and theatrical—of life in the waterside district in Charleston— Catfish Row—once the center of aristocratic life, now down-trodden as only a Southern, urban, Negro tenement district can be. The leading actors in the play were Frank Wilson as Porgy, Georgette Harvey as Maria, keeper of the cook shop, Jack Carter as Crown (played in the revival by Paul Robeson), Wesley Hill as Jake, the captain of the fishing-fleet, Rose McClendon as Serena, Evelyn Ellis as Bess, Leigh Whipper doubling in the roles of the undertaker and the crab man, A. B. Cromathière as Simon Frazier, the lawyer, Richard Huey as Mingo, and Percy Verwayne as Sporting Life. Every one of these actors had added long experience to his natural talents. Many of them had already earned the rewards of success; many of them were to be heard from soon again.

84

PORGY has become a theatre classic. In the excellent cast were Frank Wilson, Richard Huey, Wesley Hill, Percy Verwayne, Rose McClendon, Georgette Harvey, Evelyn Ellis.

85

The pattern of the action in *Porgy* was novel and exciting when it first appeared, but its high moments have all been imitated—both well and badly—often enough since then to take the bloom out of any flowering less firm. Perhaps it is because a poet gave *Porgy* its life that *Porgy* lives today. Perhaps, too, because the actors knew something of the sordid life of the characters—both bad and beautiful—that peopled it, and because there were poets among them too.

No longer was the Negro theatre "inchin' along like a po' inch worm." The success of the Negro cast in *Porgy* gave courage to a younger Harlem group who felt that the time was ripe for an honest play of life in Harlem's lower middle class. Wallace Thurman, a talented Negro writer, collaborated with William Rapp and *Harlem,* directed by Chester Erskine, was produced in 1929 with Isabell Washington playing the lead and Inez Clough as her mother. There was no romance rose-lighting the realism of *Harlem* as there had been in *Lulu Belle*. It showed a simple Southern mother, terrified and helpless as she sees her family caught in the eddies of life in a Harlem railroad flat, with its by-products of rent parties, of the "sweetback," of the "hot-stuff man," of lotteries and vice. Thurman knew his streets and his houses, the people he dealt with, their temptations, and the emotions that directed their actions. Violent and undisciplined as the play was, it left a sense of almost photographic reality.

*   *   *   *   *

Then, early in February, 1930, came a Negro play as unlike *Harlem* as it was possible to be. *The Green Pastures* was a fable play by Marc Connelly, based on stories by Roark Bradford, and produced by Laurence Rivers. It settled down at the Mansfield for 557 performances. When it finally finished its run there, it went on across the country on tour, north and south, came back to New York and played, altogether, for almost five years. Even after that, it crossed the country once more to reappear as a film. In the original cast were many familiar names: Daniel Haynes, Wesley Hill, Jesse Shipp, Homer Tutt and Tutt Whitney—and one name, a stranger to the theatre at first but soon to become most famous of all Negro theatre names—Richard B. Harrison. For almost fifty years Harrison had been a reader, chiefly of Shakespeare, on a Lyceum circuit—hoping always that the day would come when he could play Shylock on a stage. *The Green Pastures* gave him his first

THE GREEN PASTURES, by Marc Connelly had the sympathetic collaboration of Robert Edmond Jones, the Hall Johnson choir and an excellent cast headed by Richard Harrison as "de Lawd," seen above in his office. Below, the faithful on their way to the Promised Land.

87

part, and gained him international fame as 'de Lawd.' He was dead before the play returned to New York. So, too, was Wesley Hill, who had gladdened the heart of audiences as the Angel Gabriel. To see how the play looked to cultured Negroes, let Sterling Brown review *The Green Pastures:* *

"*The Green Pastures* (1930) was a miracle in the medieval sense of a biblical story presented upon the stage, and in several more important ways. It was a miracle in the length of its run, in the tenderness and reverence that Marc Connelly was able to infuse into Roark Bradford's farces, in the beautifully compelling acting of Richard Harrison, and in the perfect appropriateness of the sonorous Hall Johnson Spirituals to the narrative. Although it was called 'an attempt to present certain aspects of a living religion in the terms of its believers,' discerning critics have seen in *The Green Pastures* a statement in simple terms of the relationship of anyone and his God. . . . The frock-coat, fedora, and ten cent cigar are probably Marc Connelly's version of what Roark Bradford said was a Negro preacher's version of God, but the kindly, perplexed father of his people is like the God of the Spirituals. If the play is not accurate truth about the religion of the folk-Negro, it is movingly true to folk life. Reverend Mr. Deshee's Sunday school; the fish-fry (which, though placed in heaven, is delightfully true to the delta country) Noah's wish for the second 'kag'; young gamblers starting with 'frozen' dice; honky-tonk cabarets, magicians, country folk, city scoffers, the pure in heart, and the sinful; all of these make *The Green Pastures* a vivid résumé of folk types and folk experience. Most majestic of the folk scenes is the exodus; here in these marching people with their faces turned toward hope is a spectacle symbolic and moving. *The Green Pastures* is fantasy, but it is likewise simple profound reality."

The early 30's seemed to be full of plays about Negroes. There was *Singing the Blues* with Frank Wilson, Isabell Washington, Jack Carter, and *Savage Rhythm* with Venzuela Jones, Juano Hernandez and Ernest Whitman. There was Du Bose Heyward's *Brass Ankle* (not to be compared for quality with *Porgy*) and several effective parts for Negroes in Paul Green's *House of Connelly*.

There were others of even less importance, none of which gave the Negro theatre a clearer tone. Two plays, however, going in opposite

88   *From "Negro Poetry and Drama," by Sterling A. Brown. By permission of the author and of the editor, Alain Locke.

directions, spoke with a voice that was listened to: Hall Johnson's *Run Little Chillun*; James K. Millen's *Never No More*.

Run Little Chillun was in the line of the folk-play. It belonged in the theatre world of *The Green Pastures*. But it was not only acted by Negro actors (led by Fredi Washington, Austin Burleigh and Edna Thomas). It was written and arranged by a Negro playwright who was also a distinguished choral director. It was a theatre work, full of talent, that leaned heavily on its music choir. In *Run Little Chillun*, the Negro theatre was learning how best to use its own special advantages and its own tools. It told the story of a conflict between a new pagan cult and a Negro Baptist church in the South. Not all of the acts escaped the hackneyed, but there were two scenes fine enough to support the whole structure. One was a revival meeting with plenty of Spirituals, sung as they should be sung. The other, artificial perhaps in its dramatic substance, but equally effective, was a pagan religious orgy in a primitive forest. Frank Merlin directed the company and he showed both tact and wisdom in leaving the handling of the disciplined and accomplished singing-actors of Hall Johnson's choir in Mr. Johnson's hands. The Federal Theatre in Los Angeles later revived *Run Little Chillun* under Clarence Muse's direction, with notable success. And the play stands as an important milestone in this theatre history.

In complete contrast to *Run Little Chillun* was *Never No More* by James K. Millen. It was the first of the notable plays of social protest by means of which many playwrights have endeavored, through the visual as well as the verbal arts of the theatre, to interpret the Negro's major social and economic problems, as American citizens, to other Americans.

Mr. Millen had witnessed a lynching and was so horrified by what he saw that he felt that he must reproduce both the scene and the emotion it created so as to make such sights more nearly impossible. That was certainly a worthy dramatic motive. But the play was too consistently violent and terrifying. The exposition was too careful, too detailed, too long sustained. No fact that an audience might remember was spared them and the moment was not eased by the simplicity and pathos of Rose McClendon's acting as the Negro mother who dies vicariously while her son is dying in the flames. The audience was, if possible, too seared by its own emotion to share fully in the emotions of the characters.

Yet John Hutchens, comparing a play like *Never No More* to *Savage*

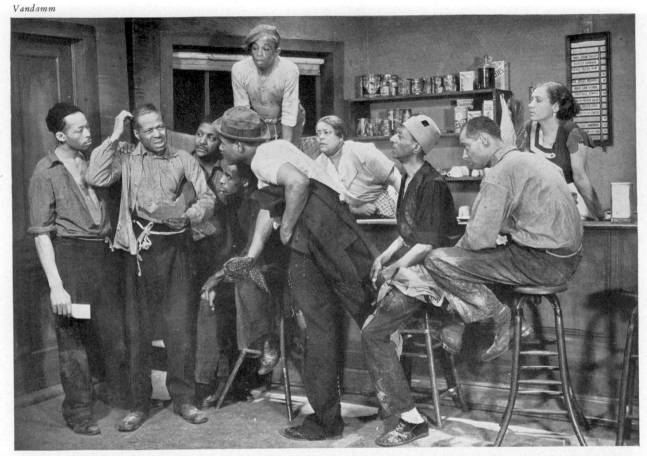

STEVEDORE by Paul Peters and George Sklar, with a cast that included many old favorites. Some of those seen in Binnie's lunchroom are Rex Ingram, Georgette Harvey, Al Watts, Leigh Whipper, Jack Carter and Edna Thomas. John Wexley's *They Shall Not Die* (below) was a "documentary" in play form.

90

Rhythm, which was a synthetic examination of the rites of self-hypnosis in the lower Mississippi swamplands, hit the nail on the head when he said: "It is an anomaly of such shows (like *Savage Rhythm*) that even their all-Negro casts, vibrant, intelligent, and sensitive to emotion as they are, have a burnt cork look about them when the pale routines are fetched out once more."

The pale routines were again not in evidence in the next protest play, *They Shall Not Die,* by John Wexley, produced by the Theatre Guild. Generally speaking, the social plays on Negro themes were—like most of the left-wing plays written during this period directly as propaganda—more sympathetic than accomplished as dramatic writing. But often what might have been merely oratorical statement was made deeply moving by eloquent acting. This was true of *They Shall Not Die,* a plea for the Scottsboro boys, then standing trial, in which—with an excellent cast headed by Claude Rains, Ruth Gordon and Frank Wilson—nine Negro boys played the protagonists. The play has been called a documentary in play form, and in its best scenes it was effective in almost the same way as a well-made documentary film. But the firmest play of the early group was undoubtedly *Stevedore,* by George Sklar and Paul Peters, which turned upon the relation of the Negro to the labor union, to the terrors attendant upon unemployment, and to racial cooperation. The cast was made up of many of the theatre's oldest friends: Rex Ingram as Black Snake, Jack Carter as Lonnie Thompson, Georgette Harvey as Binnie, Edna Thomas as Ruby Oxley, Leigh Whipper as Jim Veal. *Stevedore* was produced at the Civic Repertory Theatre by Theatre Union, Inc., and it was the best production made by that group. Instead of trying to do too many things at once it confined its material fairly closely to its own theme, namely that the freedom to work on equal terms with other men is any man's first freedom. It applied this especially, of course, to the Negro laborer, to the stevedores who had learned to work with men like Lonnie Thompson, whose class consciousness was stronger even than his feeling for race and who was "framed" by "higher-ups" to get him out of the way. The group scenes especially—in Binnie's lunch room and on the docks where a ship was being loaded—were notably effective, in settings by Sointu Syrjala. And the fact that the men and women were used as individuals rather than as types gave the actors a rich opportunity for characterization.

Apart from dramas that were conventional in form, even when they had fresh material, the year 1934 had several significant entries. The first of these was *Four Saints in Three Acts*. The composer and author of *Four Saints*, Virgil Thomson and Gertrude Stein, called *Four Saints* an opera to be sung. Actually, it was a sung-dance, striking and original in both form and treatment. It had an extraordinary Negro cast, unified in John Houseman's production, and it was altogether successful. It came at the height of the season, in February when theatre tickets are always in demand. It was well suited to an audience looking for the unusual, and it got a large and appreciative house. Its settings of oil cloth and gauze and cellophane, the costumes of lace and simulated gold cloths were lovely to look at—the work of Florine Stettheimer, who was known as a painter, not as a theatre artist. The words made little sense, but they were colorful and evocative and lent themselves to song. The music was reminiscent but had an effective melodic and dramatic line that maintained the mood of solemn nonsense. The stylized movement was in the hands of the talented young English choreographer, Frederick Ashton, and was handled to perfection. Edward Matthews in the leading role of St. Ignatius, with his beautiful singing, and his steady, solemnly comic attitude and movement, was the great artist of the occasion. The two lovely Saints Theresa, Bruce Howard and Beatrice Robinson-Wayne, and the St. Chavez (John Diggs) shared the honors with him if, indeed, every member of the company may not be said to have shared them. *Four Saints* was an artistic and social event and yet, if the memory it left were less delightful, it might easily be passed over here as coming from nowhere and adding little that has a bearing on the story of the Negro in the American theatre.

The next event was at almost the farthest extreme from *Four Saints* in background, authorship, production, and audience appeal. It was *Kykunkor*, called an African dance-opera by Asadata Dafora (Horton). It was not performed in a theatre—not at first, that is—but in a little hall on East 23rd Street with a stage so small that you could almost touch the rear from the front row, and with a floor that trembled when the native drummers started beating out their rhythms and that shook violently when the dance of the Witch Doctor began. *Kykunkor* was an adaptation of an African ritual, in dance, costume and music, and it created such an impression of faithfulness to form and material and opened up so many new—yet age-old—possibilities in music and dance,

FOUR SAINTS IN THREE ACTS, by Gertrude Stein and Virgil Thomson, divided the honors about evenly between the authors, the director (John Houseman), the choreographer (Frederick Ashton), the singing actors and dancing chorus. Edward Matthews played Saint Ignatius; John Diggs, Saint Chavez; and Bruce Howard and Beatrice Robinson-Wayne, the Saints Theresa.

that it quickly drummed and danced its way to public attention, moved uptown, became the base of an African dance unit of the Federal Theatre Project and has since developed a steadily growing interest in native African ritual forms. *Kykunkor* reminded many of those older folk who had seen the dancers from Dahomey at the Chicago World's Fair in 1893 of what Henry Krehbiel, with his perceptive eye and pen wrote of them at that time:

"Berlioz in his supremest effort with his army of drummers produced nothing to compare in artistic interest with their harmonious drumming. . . . The fundamental effect was a combination of double and triple time, the former kept by the singers, the latter by the drummers, but it is impossible to convey the idea of the wealth of detail achieved by the drummers by means of exchange of the rhythms, syncopation of both simultaneously, and dynamic devices."

The third candidate for public approval that year fell half-way between the folk-play and the play of protest. It was Paul Green's drama of shantytown life, called *Roll, Sweet Chariot,* and it lasted only seven performances. Most of the critics, white and Negro alike, saw only its strangeness and failed to see that it was, in many ways, theatrically prophetic. Yet *Roll, Sweet Chariot* was definitely the forerunner of a long line of music-plays that were happily coming up—plays like *Johnny Johnson, Knickerbocker Holiday,* and even *Oklahoma!*. Paul Green has done as much as any man to dilate the region of the American theatre as a whole, and this was one of his important adventures.

For years there had been talk and writing of the possibility of modern plays that would use their people and their themes as the Elizabethans did, not singly but together, weaving the individual stories into a pattern of character and action, adding to all the strength of each. For years we had been looking forward to the time when someone would make a play of words and music in which the music should be as integral a part of the play's sound and meaning as the words. *Roll, Sweet Chariot,* with Dolphe Martin's dramatic music, achieved much of this. It was about a heterogeneous group of Negroes that live in or hang around a boarding house in a run-down settlement that is invaded by a steam roller, and about the building of a new road that threatens the isolation of the wretched, inchoate community. It used every well-tried element of theatrical emotion—love and crime, jealousy and fear, the presence of poverty and the hope of wealth, pistols, the police, the chain gang. It

94

THE KING in an African opera, *Kykunkor*, presented by Asadata Dafora
(Horton) as a part of a program of research in African arts which aims to
place a racial foundation under modern American Negro dance and music,
and also to stress the aesthetic values of native traditions and rituals.

95

blended them all through music and the poetry of words, action and fine acting, so that they became humanly exciting and dramatically satisfying and stimulating.

No large group of actors, except Negroes, could have moved as this cast, headed by Frank Wilson, Rose McClendon and Warren Coleman, did, from speech to chant, from chant to song, and back again to direct speech without a break in the rhythm of performance. That alone was a major theatre accomplishment. Today it would not pass unnoticed.

A play made from a story by one of the most talented Negro poets, Langston Hughes, was produced in 1935. It was titled *Mulatto* and its run was the longest on Broadway enjoyed by any play of Negro authorship up to that time. Its main theme was a young mulatto's hatred of his white father and it lent itself to all the sensational elements involved. *Mulatto* carried the name of Martin Jones as Hughes' collaborator and what has been said of it seems credible: namely that the play was rewritten during Hughes' absence and that he himself was unhappy over the result. It had neither the penetration nor the beauty of his poetic work, nor the gay humor and theatre values of his comedies *When the Jack Hollers* and *Little Ham*, produced over and over again with great success by the Gilpin Players of Karamu House in Cleveland.

Mulatto was Rose McClendon's last Broadway performance before she died. And her death emphasized again the many changes for the better that had come over the Negro's position, even in a single actor's lifetime. There was still a long distance to go, but it could be measured by the distance covered.

It was only twenty-five years since Bert Williams was invited to join the *Follies* and soon became the first featured Negro player in a white show. It was a full ten years later (1920) when Charles Gilpin came to fame as The Emperor Jones. In 1921, *Shuffle Along* brought down its bandwagon full of stars; in 1924, Paul Robeson in *All God's Chillun Got Wings*. In 1926, *In Abraham's Bosom* won the Pulitzer prize, and, through his acting in the name part, Jules Bledsoe gained the role of Joe in the next year's *Showboat*, singing "Old Man River" through 572 Broadway performances. That same year *Porgy*, and Florence Mills in *Blackbirds*; in 1928, more *Blackbirds* with Bill Robinson. In 1929, again a Pulitzer award, this time for *The Green Pastures* with Richard B. Harrison. By 1933, good parts for Negroes in many plays, and the first

96

TONIEA MASSAQUOI, a young Liberian dancer, wood-carver and architectural designer, who used the name of Frank Roberts when he danced at the Radio City Dance International and with the Creative Dance Unit of Hampton Institute. His work, both in old rituals and in modern forms, is unlike Oriental or modern Western dance, but has its own free African character and clear sense of beauty.

97

important play by a Negro writer and composer, Hall Johnson's *Run Little Chillun.* 1934 brought Negro offerings as varied as *Four Saints in Three Acts, Stevedore* and *Kykunkor.* . . .

In Harlem, they founded the Rose McClendon Players to carry on her traditions. If you watched them, you could see a new Negro theatre forming, a new line of Negro actors coming up, one at a time, so that you hardly noticed them until the new line was already there.

And then came *Porgy and Bess*! And all New York, and soon all of America, sat up and listened to the work which has been rightly accorded the title of the first native American folk opera. DuBose Heyward made the script from the play which he and his wife, Dorothy Heyward, had in turn dramatized from DuBose Heyward's novel *Porgy.* The music was by George Gershwin. On the opening night he himself was in the orchestra pit wielding the conductor's baton. The setting was the familiar one that Cleon Throckmorton had created for the play and which had become a theatre classic. It seemed at once as though the line that ran straight on the one hand from *The Rider of Dreams, The Emperor Jones, Porgy* and *The Green Pastures,* and, on the musical side, from *Shuffle Along, Blackbirds,* to *Run Little Chillun* finally met in this work. The score—inventive, melodious, modern and full of vigor—seemed to flow on without a halt. Gershwin's great, free talent reached its height in *Porgy and Bess,* and fortunately the composer and the author had a cast remarkably well-fitted to interpret their work in action. Todd Duncan came up from a professor's chair at Howard University to win a veritable triumph as the crippled Porgy. Anne Wiggins Brown was Bess (Etta Moten in the revival), and Ruby Elzy, Serena. Edward Matthews (remembered especially from *Four Saints in Three Acts*) was Jake. John W. Bubbles played Sporting Life (the part Avon Long played in the 1942 revival). Abbie Mitchell was Clara (Harriet Jackson in 1942); Georgette Harvey was Maria, as she had been in the play; J. Rosamond Johnson was Frazier. Singing Gershwin's difficult music was no small mastery for the singing-actors and it is to them, as well as to the composer, that the credit goes for having made some of the songs, like "Summertime" and Porgy's "I Got Plenty of Nothin'," a part of our familiar musical literature.

Porgy and Bess has toured the country, has been revived with even greater success than in its first production, has toured the country again,

PORGY AND BESS, generally credited with being the first American folk opera.

has been made into a concert work with orchestration by R. Russell Bennett, is announced for another revival and shows no sign of losing favor in the public ear and eye. In fact, except in the material matters of production rights and royalties, it is, one might say, "in the public domain."

It is characteristic of this whole theatre story that the first complete achievement in this field, the first important native opera on a Negro theme, with music in the Negro idiom, should be written and composed by white men. So far, all the best plays of Negro life, except perhaps Hall Johnson's *Run Little Chillun,* had been written by white men—experienced writers like Paul Green, DuBose Heyward, Marc Connelly.

So too, white composers were the first to explore the serious potentialities of jazz. But it soon became evident that this precedence in time was only a matter of perspective. Negro musicians were too close to their folk rhythms to recognize the full possibilities for development at once, but today Negro jazz composers are second to none. And, given a clear field in the theatre, there is good evidence from the young talents already stirring that we will not have to wait overlong for first-rate plays of Negro life by Negroes and for an opera with Negro composer and librettist.

Genius, we have come to recognize, is a matter of the individual and not the race. But even a genius needs full opportunity and long association to learn the elaborate techniques of the theatre. He needs to be as much at home in theatre-ways as in folkways and the ways of race. And after that the whole theatre experience must be "recollected in tranquillity" before the impulse for dramatic creation begins, before a man is ready to face all the complex relationships involved in play production, the strains of rehearsal, the violence of critical reaction. And for the Negro dramatist who has been, and in many places still is, a stranger in theatre audiences this is an added barrier.

Fortunately for our literature as a whole, the material for many kinds of Negro drama—from folk comedy to tragedy—falls easily within a poet's ken and Negro poets, although not many of them are writing plays as yet, seem to turn spontaneously toward the dramatic, in form or content, in situation, or character, or mood. It would be a simple thing for a fine theatre to woo them. If you regard the theatre as the most democratic, forceful and interpretative of the arts, you cannot help envying the many play-kernels that are buried in short poems.

100

There is the protagonist of tragedy, of whom Countee Cullen sang in "Heritage": *

> All day long and all night through
> One thing only must I do:
> Quench my pride and cool my blood,
> Lest I perish in the flood.
> Lest a hidden ember set
> Timber that I thought was wet
> Burning like the driest flax,
> Melting like the merest wax.

And there is his opposite, "Sporting Beasley," whom Sterling Brown depicts so lovingly, and who would make such a strutting hero for a Harlem dance fantasy written for Avon Long: **

> Good Glory, give a look at Sporting Beasley
> Strutting, oh my Lord.
>
> Tophat cocked one side his bulldog head,
> Striped four-in-hand, and in his buttonhole
> A red carnation; Prince Albert coat
> Form-fitting, corset like; vest snugly filled,
> Gray morning trousers, spotless and full-flowing,
> White spats and a cane.
>
> Step it, Mr. Beasley, oh step it till the sun goes down.
>
> .   .   .   .   .
>
> Oh Jesus, when this brother's bill falls due,
> When he steps off the chariot
> And flicks the dust from his patent leathers with his silk hand-
>   kerchief,
> When he stands in front of the jasper gates, patting his tie,
> And then paces in
> Cane and knees working like well-oiled slow-timed pistons;
>
> Lord help us, give a *look* at him.
>
> Don't make him dress up in no night gown, Lord.
> Don't put no fuss and feathers on his shoulders, Lord.
>
> Let him know it's heaven.
> Let him keep his hat, his vest, his elkstooth, and everything.
>
> Let him have his spats and cane
> Let him have his spats and cane.

*From "Color," by Countee Cullen, copyrighted 1925 by Harper and Brothers, Pub-
lishers, and printed with their permission.
**From "Sporting Beasley," in the volume "Southern Road," by Sterling A. Brown.
With permission of the author and of the publishers, Harcourt, Brace and Company. (Copyright 1932.)

And between the two, the lonely lad of Robert Hayden's "Bacchanal": *

> Gonna git high,
> High's a Georgia pine,
> Can't laugh,
> Don't wanna cry:
> Gonna git high.
>
> Factory closed this mawnin,
> Done drawed that last full pay;
> One of these Hastings studs
> Done coaxed ma brown away.
>
> A little likker,
> O a little gin
> Makes you fergit
> The fix you in.
>
> What the hell's the use'n
> Miseryin on? . . .
> Wonder what I'll do when
> My lush-money's gone.
>
> There must be joy,
> There's gotta be joy somewhere
> For a po colored boy
> This side the sky.
>
> Gonna git high.

And the loveliest, and most clearly theatre of all, perhaps, yet not written either as drama or as poetry, but as a short story by a young scientist, "Miss Cynthie" by Rudolph Fisher: **Everybody, black and white in her little Southern village, has called her Miss Cynthie during most of the seventy years of her life. So, too, her beloved grandson, whom she has just come to New York to visit. David was a boy of parts when she sent him North to get an education so he could become a doctor; if not a body doctor, then a tooth doctor; if not a tooth doctor, then a foot doctor; if not a foot doctor, then an undertaker so he would still be helping to do the Lord's work. She sent him with only one admonition: Whatever you do, do like a church steeple: aim high and go straight.

*From "Bacchanal," by Robert Hayden, with the author's permission.
**"Miss Cynthie," by Rudolph Fisher. By permission of "Story Magazine," which first printed it in the issue of June, 1933.

Miss Cynthie does not know just what David has actually been doing, but she knows he has been successful, for he has fine clothes and a sky-blue roadster in which he drives her proudly from Grand Central Station up to Harlem where the big churches warm her heart. In the evening, however, it is not to church they go, but to a box at the Lafayette Theatre where Miss Cynthie sees a song-and-dance show that rips into her very soul—those raucous songs, that cotton-picking chorus dancing in their abbreviated shorts and legs naked to the thigh!

There is an intermission. David leaves her. Another act, another chorus, and out through the midst of them comes her David in blue satin overalls with a green bandana and patent-leather shoes. He is singing, too, and dancing too, and the audience goes wild with pleasure. Miss Cynthie, the epitome of supreme failure, watches this boy whom she had brought up in the church disporting himself for a sin-sick mob of lost souls, not one of whom probably cared to know of God's loving kindness. Then a sound catches her ear, the familiar rhythm of her own song that she had sung to David years and years ago. He is singing it and tapping it out:

> Oh, I danced with the gal' with the hole in her stockin',
> And her toe kep' a'kickin' and her heel kep' a'knockin'
> "Come up, Jesse, and get a drink o' gin,
> Cause you near to the heaven as you'll ever get ag'in."

David smiles at Miss Cynthie. She listens as in a trance, as he goes on:

> Then I danced with the gal with the dimple in her cheek—
> An' if she'd kep' a-smilin', I'd a' danced for a week—

Miss Cynthie sees the audience smiling now, a happy smile, and she whispers, "Bless my soul! They didn' mean nothin' . . . . they jes' didn' see no harm in it."

Then David—Dave Tapper, king of tappers in Harlem and Broadway—tries to share his applause with Miss Cynthie and to give her a rose that someone has thrown to him. Smiling, she reprimands him:

"Keep it, you fool. Where's yo' manners—givin' 'way what somebody give you?"

David grins: "Take it, tyro. What you tryin' to do—crab my act?"

As the audience files out, Miss Cynthie's foot continues patting time

AVON LONG, who first came to attention as Sporting Life in the revival of *Porgy and Bess.* Someone who saw his dancing in *Beggar's Holiday* described it thus: "He dances like a feather in the wind. He is bent over at your right hand and then suddenly he is at your left and you haven't seen him go."

to the orchestra's jazz recessional. She is thinking: "God moves in a mysterious way."

"Miss Cynthie" was first published in "Story Magazine" in 1933 (the year before Rudolph Fisher died at 37) and was reprinted in Edward O'Brien's anthology of the year's best stories. If you read it you will find that it does two things: it gives a clearer understanding of the kinetic enjoyment that you get from Bill Robinson's dancing. It proves beyond a doubt how greatly the man who wrote it—who in a few pages could create the scene, round out the characters, tell the luminous story, and stir that happy sadness around your heart—how greatly that man might have enriched our theatre if the theatre had opened wide its doors. Our prejudices are an expensive luxury.

Vandamm

LOUIS ARMSTRONG brought his "hot jazz" trumpet to Broadway as Bottom in Swingin' the Dream, *an adaptation of* A Midsummer Night's Dream.

7

THE FEDERAL THEATRE AND AFTER

THE FEDERAL THEATRE was started in 1935 as a part of the New Deal's broad effort to relieve depression unemployment by paid work in a man's chosen field rather than by a dole. It wisely took into account the fact that the concentration of theatres in a few big cities—and especially in New York—had never permitted enough people and enough kinds of people through the country to share the theatre experience. So it was understood that a major purpose of the project was to "offer to the people access to the arts and tools of a civilization which they themselves are helping to make." Such a theatre was expected to be "at once an illustration and a bulwark of the democratic form of government." The country was divided into regions; the theatre regions subdivided under directors. It was agreed that the choice of plays would be left to the directors to suit the needs of their varied posts with the suggestion that everywhere emphasis should be placed on new American plays, classical plays, children's plays and a special program for Negro companies.

No part of the Federal Theatre brought more ample returns to the project itself than did the Negro units and, conversely, no American theatre project (except perhaps the Lafayette Theatre during its long history) has meant more to Negro players and other theatre artists than the Federal Theatre did. The audience for Negro theatres in other parts of the country had always remained uncertain, in numbers and in taste;

106

TURPENTINE was a modern, realistic labor play by J. A. Smith and Peter Morell, staged by the New York Federal Theatre unit, with Charlie Taylor, Gus Smith, Louis Sharp, Thurman Jackson in the cast. Together with classics like *Macbeth*, folkplays like *Run Little Chillun*, modern historical dramas like William DuBois' *Haiti*, it illustrates the wide range of Federal Theatre drama, production method and performance.

the Harlem theatre had always been too poor to support even its most talented group steadily over long periods. The best-known Negro actors had too much off-time to fill with other, less-congenial jobs. Negro playwrights, unwelcome in most theatre audiences, had no opportunity to learn their trade by watching the work of experienced playwrights in performance. Even the audiences had no chance to grow theatre-loving and theatre-wise. The Federal Theatre on the other hand welcomed its Negro audiences and gave its actors and technicians work and wages, gave them money for fresh designs and productions, and plenty of time for rehearsals. Moreover, it encouraged initiative, invention and experiment. In spite of all its professional, economic and political handicaps, the Federal Theatre did a big and an important job.

There were enterprising Negro units in New York, Seattle, Hartford, Philadelphia, Newark, Los Angeles, Boston, Birmingham, San Francisco and other cities. A survey of Negro employment on the project (in February, 1939) showed 851 Negro personnel and seventy-five plays produced by their groups alone. Moreover, the Federal Theatre offered Negroes excellent parts in plays by other units like the Living Newspaper *One-Third of a Nation*, or Orson Welles' far-heralded *Doctor Faustus* in which Jack Carter played Mephistopheles.

Los Angeles was among the most active areas. There Hall Johnson's *Run Little Chillun* ran for almost a year to enthusiastic houses. Seattle was a challenge with an adventurous program that ranged from *Lysistrata* and *The Taming of the Shrew* to *Androcles and the Lion, In Abraham's Bosom, Noah, Stevedore* and Theodore Browne's new play *Natural Man*. Chicago was perhaps New York's closest competitor, but Philadelphia, Hartford and other cities were not far behind.

In New York the unit was fortunate in securing the Lafayette Theatre as its center of action. On Rose McClendon's advice, and with the enthusiastic support of the group, John Houseman was selected as the first director since there were few Negroes who had had enough experience in direction to do their company full justice. The New York unit was, in many ways, a reflection of life in New York City. It was "everything in excess." It had fine talents, a diversity of taste and desire, a wide range of productions. It had at its disposal a host of young men and women, many of them gifted, who had never had a chance, and a host of older folk whose only reason for being in the theatre was that they had once been there and could today find work nowhere else. As

108

EDNA THOMAS as Lady Macbeth reached the high point of a long and varied career. The entire Federal Theatre production of *Macbeth* is often spoken of as the peak of the Harlem Negro unit. Orson Welles and John Houseman prepared the version and directed the production. Canada Lee played Banquo. Jack Carter, as Macbeth, added to the reputation he had made as Lonnie in *Stevedore*. Nat Karson made the brilliant designs, one of which is reproduced below.

a result the level of production was uneven but the best of it was very good and the second-best was as good as much of Broadway.

The New York Negro unit produced every kind of play—classics in straight and re-made versions, well-known modern plays, musicals and dance-dramas. They wrote and produced new plays by and about Negroes, like Frank Wilson's *Walk Together Children,* a dramatization of Rudolph Fisher's detective story *Conjur' Man Dies,* and *Turpentine* by J. A. Smith and Peter Morrell, which aimed at vivifying for a larger public the desperate struggle of the Negro laborer in the turpentine swamps of Florida. They delved into the noblest pages of Negro history to produce one of the most colorful of their plays, *Haiti,* by William DuBois, a melodrama of the historic struggle in which Toussaint L'Ouverture led the West Indians against their French overlords in 1802. Louis Sharp played Toussaint L'Ouverture; Rex Ingram, Christophe; Alvin Childress, Jacques; and Canada Lee (an old name to vaudeville but new to most other audiences) played Bertram.

The Harlem *Macbeth* is theatre legend today. It was a torrid version of Shakespeare's tale with suitable tropical settings by Nat Karson. Edna Thomas was Lady Macbeth; Jack Carter, Macbeth; and Canada Lee, Banquo. Orson Welles and John Houseman directed this *Macbeth,* or, one could more fairly say, created it. They made it a jungle tragedy of black ambition. They used flashing lights and pounding drums to add emphasis to the movement of the crowds and to heighten the emotions of the audience. It was, as someone said, "the Emperor Jones gone beautifully mad" but it certainly satisfied an audience need at the moment, for, in Harlem and on tour, over a hundred thousand people saw this *Macbeth* and revelled in it.

For many years the chief disciples of the form of music we now know as "hot jazz" came from Chicago. It was quite to be expected, therefore, that the best example of the new madness in the Federal Theatre should also come from Chicago, as it did in the form of the *Swing Mikado,* all swing and heat and feathers and laughter. This Chicago variant of Gilbert and Sullivan, directed by Harry Minturn, was so successful that it caught the envious eye of the commercial theatre. In accordance with government regulations, the Federal Theatre was obliged to sell it. This quite naturally encouraged other swing productions not under Federal Theatre auspices. The first of these was called *The Hot Mikado* produced by Michael Todd with Bill Robinson in the lead. It was gorgeously capar-

110

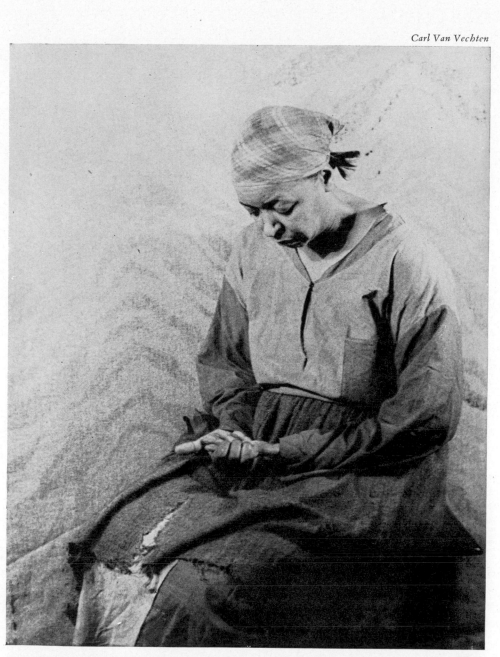

MAMBA'S DAUGHTERS, by DuBose and Dorothy Heyward, gave Ethel Waters, as Hagar, her first important role as a dramatic actress. After many successful years as a night-club and musical comedy singer she fully met the challenge of the changed medium. With her in the cast were Georgette Harvey as Mamba, and Fredi Washington as Hagar's daughter.

isoned, and it danced its way into the World's Fair, but somehow it lacked the verve and charm of the *Swing Mikado*. The second was *Swingin' the Dream* which capitalized on the success accorded to *Macbeth* and the *Swing Mikado* with Maxine Sullivan's alluring voice, Louis Armstrong's magic trumpet, Butterfly McQueen as Puck, Oscar Polk as Flute and Juano Hernandez as Oberon.

When the Federal Theatre was closed by act of Congress, the Negro units left more of value behind them than the memory of much good acting, inventive production and various artistic, as well as commercial, successes. They left actors with new assurance of their talent, directors and young playwrights strengthened by experience and hope. They left a consciousness of what they could really do, given the opportunity.

*   *   *   *   *

Guthrie McClintic may have seen Ethel Waters' possibilities as a dramatic actress when she played in *Androcles and the Lion* with the Federal Theatre, in a cast with Edna Thomas, Dooley Wilson and Daniel Haynes. Or it may have been simply Mr. McClintic's directorial instinct that led him to offer her the role of Hagar in Dorothy and DuBose Heyward's *Mamba's Daughters*. Whatever it was, it established Ethel Waters in a position which no other Negro actress had yet achieved. Even Rose McClendon, although she had many opportunities to contribute to the success of good plays, had never had a role commensurate with her talents. What made Ethel Waters' success the more remarkable was that, with all her long experience, she had never lost the haunting folk quality that distinguished both her acting and her singing from the beginning.

Like most of the important Negro players, both actors and actresses, Ethel Waters came up the hard way. Perhaps her way was even a little harder and a little longer than that of some of her fellows. She remembers singing the "St. Louis Blues" at the Lincoln Theatre in Harlem for nine dollars a week. She thought it was lucky when she secured an engagement to sing in a Harlem night club, and most fortunate when she took Florence Mills' place, for a while, as the lead in the *Plantation Revue*. An adventurous producer in 1929 had given her the lead in a revue called *Africana* where she showed off to advantage. *Africana* led to more important engagements. Ethel Waters was featured with Clifton Webb and Helen Broderick in *As Thousands Cheer* and won high favor with her singing in *At Home Abroad*. But there were empty days before

112

Mamba's Daughters gave her her great chance. Like *Oklahoma!* or *The Green Pastures* it was one of those rare plays in which the authors, the actors, the director and the designer (in this case Perry Watkins) form a unit of understanding and expression. The story centered around the women of three generations, devastatingly poor, but proud, devoted, ambitious. Mamba was played by Georgette Harvey; her daughter Hagar by Ethel Waters; and Hagar's daughter by Fredi Washington. Fredi is a beautiful child and a talented singer; mother and grandmother live and work for her alone. Hagar is a great, strong woman, gentle as a child until she is deeply stirred and then capable of any violence. Sin, desertion, murder crowd in on the quiet home and the whole gamut of emotions they evoke falls to Ethel Waters to express. There was no critical doubt that she mastered the part completely. And yet the next year she could turn from that difficult dramatic role, which demanded supreme concentration of body and spirit, to play with gaiety and relaxed vitality the lead in the bright fantasy *Cabin in the Sky*. There are not many actresses, or actors either, who could make so great a transition so easily and so well.

Vinton Freedley produced *Cabin in the Sky*, a "minor theatre miracle of happy collaboration," and, it might be added, of generous casting and production. The success of *Cabin in the Sky* was no accident. The book was by Lynn Root, the score by Vernon Duke, the lyrics by John Latouche, the settings by Boris Aronson. The story was woven around Little Joe who, although he had died in sin, was fortunate in having a wife strong enough to get him another life in which to redeem himself. Dooley Wilson played the crapshootin', razor-pullin' Little Joe. Rex Ingram was Lucifer, Jr., the villain of the piece; Todd Duncan, who sang the chief arias, was the Lawd's General; J. Rosamond Johnson led his choir in holy songs; Katherine Dunham as the Scarlet Woman, with her dancers, added their movement and charm. What more could anyone want?

Cabin in the Sky was still playing when Orson Welles and John Houseman brought to the St. James Theatre a dramatization, by Paul Green and Richard Wright, of Wright's brilliant and terrifying novel of Negro life in Chicago slums, *Native Son*. When it was rumored that *Native Son* was coming into the theatre, many people shook their heads, even more violently than they had about every realistic play of Negro life since *The Nigger*. Surely, they said, *Native Son* was out of bounds.

113

CANADA LEE as Bigger Thomas in the Richard Wright-Paul Green dramatization of Wright's stirring novel of the shattering effect of a Chicago slum on a man's character. The distance between the Cakewalk and *Native Son* is the measure of the Negro's theatre progress in fifty years.

But not at all. The commercial theatre sometimes—in fact, far too often—gulps hard over new ideas or new forms when they are presented in what is strangely named "legitimate drama"; that is, drama that kneads some thoughtfulness into its action. But give a theatre audience the roughest possible material and if it is fast-moving, well acted and directed and has a heavy coating—either farce or melodrama—and nine chances out of ten the theatre will swallow it without strain.

It would have been a strange theatre indeed that refused anything as powerful as *Native Son*, acted by a man as perfect for the part as Canada Lee. Bigger Thomas, in Mr. Lee's interpretation, is always both a real man and a symbol. He is the stored-up resentment of a powerful Negro against all the elements in society that have frustrated him and denied him life, liberty and the pursuit of happiness. Even his love for his mother and his girl friend turn to violence and hate. Murder belongs to the pattern of his life and when he is finally arrested and brought to trial, his trial makes the world he lives in his codefendant. It is always difficult to find roles suited to a man of Canada Lee's scale and power but *Native Son* was made to his measure and he met every opportunity the play offered. Even in the spots where the play faltered in its departure from the novel, Canada Lee filled in the lights and shadows. *Native Son* had a very real effect on the social conscience of its audience, and the theatre waits for a play by Richard Wright that shall be written even more closely to the pattern of the theatre.

8

YESTERDAY AND TODAY

THE STORY of the Negro-American actor, Ira Aldridge, who, a century ago, traveled across Europe triumphantly playing the classics, and especially *Othello,* highlights the first chapter of this history. It is balanced here, in the last chapter, by the story of another American Negro, Paul Robeson, playing *Othello* happily and with great success in his native land. It has often been said that there is marked similarity between the lives of these two men. Actually there seems to be little. Both were the children of earnest, educated, minister fathers who wished the best for their sons and who counted education among the generating influences toward the best. Both Aldridge and Robeson had the advantage—as actors—of magnificent presence and of voices of unusual range, expressiveness and flexibility. But there the resemblance seems to end. Aldridge was a born man of the theatre; for Robeson the theatre was a secondary interest. His life's devotion was not, like Aldridge's, to his art, but to his race. His aim was to reach out to his people, and—for his people—to other men through the medium which came to him most naturally, song. Actually the theatre has pursued Robeson as most other actors are obliged to pursue the theatre.

Robeson's youth was sunlit by his father's love, companionship and inspiration. He was one of the first Negroes to be admitted to Rutgers. He was a brilliant student, a leader in athletics and very popular. His father died before Paul had finished his course but he had seen him well

PAUL ROBESON as Othello in the Theatre Guild's production of Shakespeare's tragedy, which played 296 performances on Broadway.

117

on the way to most of the honors that college afforded. When Robeson graduated he had made Phi Beta Kappa, had twelve athletic letters, been elected to Cap and Skull (a senior society made up of men who best represent the ideals of the college) had delivered the commencement oration, and had been chosen by Walter Camp as end on his all-American football team.

Robeson's father had wanted him to be either a minister or a lawyer, and the year Paul Robeson graduated he settled in Harlem and entered the Columbia Law School. But somehow a career at the bar never looked like a goal to Robeson although he graduated with credit and secured a good opening in the District Attorney's office. Even at this time the theatre, with good pay for short spurts, began to tease. An amateur performance of *Simon the Cyrenian* in Harlem led to *Taboo* on Broadway; to the same role in London, opposite Mrs. Pat Campbell who told him he should begin to be thinking about *Othello*. A few small parts here and there, and then the offer from the Provincetown to play the lead in *All God's Chillun Got Wings*. The concerts of Spirituals and work-songs that won both the critics and the audience; a revival of *The Emperor Jones*, Joe in the New York revival of *Showboat* and in London, *The Emperor Jones* in Berlin, and then, in 1930, *Othello* in London. Long before this critics had written enthusiastically of the eloquence of Robeson's acting; the effect it created as 'of a soul bombarded by thunder and torn by lightning.' Yet neither the praise of critics nor the applause of audiences could make Robeson's place in the theatre quite real to him.

Robeson is a modest man and yet it was not altogether modesty that created the gulf between him and his sense of theatre achievement. Even the London *Othello,* in which he played to Maurice Browne's Iago, Peggy Ashcroft's Desdemona, Sybil Thorndike's Emilia, seemed to him, in spite of its considerable success, "static"; as indeed it was. There were too many acting methods represented; the settings and costumes were too decorative; Robeson was obviously not entirely at home either in the part or in his clothes. But London's response to him as a man and an artist was welcome to Robeson, and he spent most of the next ten years in England and in Russia, singing, studying peoples, their languages and especially their folk songs. By the end of that time he knew both the world and himself better. And as he looked back on *Othello* the play began to take on new meaning. It was no longer a study of individual

118

jealousy but of the price men pay for separateness and racial antagonism.

Othello had come well within the orbit of Robeson's personal and social philosophy. By that time, too, it seemed to him that he could help the cause of the Negro in the United States better by being closer to it, so he came home, and shortly, with a new eagerness, met the opportunity offered by Cheryl Crawford and Margaret Webster to play *Othello* at Brattle Hall in Cambridge with José Ferrer as Iago and Uta Hagen as Desdemona. The play had mixed but generally favorable notices and went on to play again at Princeton. Yet neither to Miss Webster, as director, nor to Robeson did it seem ready for New York. For the first time Robeson felt the need to be completely on the inside of a part, and especially of this part, and to be at one with it before he played it again. *Othello* was presented in New York by the Theatre Guild more than a year later, on October 19, 1943, and broke all records for the performance of this tragedy. A long, successful tour tells much the rest of the story.

The quality of Robeson's performance naturally aroused comparison with other great Othellos. It recalled what Théophile Gautier said of Ira Aldridge, whom Gautier saw in St. Petersburg in 1863. He was, Gautier says, "Othello himself, as Shakespeare has created him." He was "quiet, reserved, classic, majestic" without the "fiery, disordered, rather barbaric style" of Edmund Kean. This comes close to a description of Robeson's characterization. He might have been the man of whom Lodovico spoke when he asked Iago:

> Is this the noble Moor whom our full senate
> Call all in all sufficient? This the nature
> Whom passion could not shake? Whose solid virtue
> The shot of accident, nor dart of chance
> Could neither graze nor pierce?

There was something less than savage madness in his frenzies. When it came to the climax you did not quite believe what he had said much earlier, and with less cause:

> My blood begins my safer guides to rule,
> And passion, having my best judgment collied,
> Assays to lead the way: if I once stir,
> Or do but lift this arm, the best of you
> Shall sink in my rebuke.

But that restraint was a small failing, if failing it was, in a performance that was marked by great dignity, by love that touched the realm of majesty, and by a vocal beauty and expressiveness that matched the deep penetration of Shakespeare's lines. When Robeson said:

> . . . . I fetch my life and being
> From men of royal seige, and my demerits
> May speak unbonnetted to as proud a fortune
> As this that I have reached.

or when he ended his speech to the Senate:

> She loved me for the dangers I had pass'd,
> And I loved her that she did pity them.

you could say again, as Gautier said of Aldridge, this was "Othello himself, as Shakespeare has created him."

*   *   *   *   *

As a Christmas present to New York theatregoers in 1943, Billy Rose, with his usual fanfare, brought to the Broadway Theatre a musical play in two acts. The offering was called *Carmen Jones* by Oscar Hammerstein II, an adaptation of *Carmen*, with Bizet's music, and certain orchestral arrangements by R. Russell Bennett. It was staged by Hazzard Short; the settings were by Howard Bay; costumes by Raoul Pène duBois. There was nothing but the opera's title to indicate that this was a transformation of Merimée's story about a gypsy tobacco girl and her toreador lover into the story of a girl-worker in a southern parachute factory, an MP from a nearby camp and Husky Miller, a prize fighter. And yet if you knew how to read the signs you knew that this was to be a Negro show, although Robert Shaw of the Collegiate Choir was directing the choral singing instead of Hall Johnson or Eva Jesseye, and Eugene Loring was patterning the dances held securely to Bizet's music. There were no familiar names among the actors but the libretto told a Negro story, in the Negro idiom, with Negro interpreters, yet with little else of the 'racial' to stand between the opera and the audience.

The measure of *Carmen Jones'* success was not only the length of its run (231 performances), not only the critical approval it had—as a libretto, a production, a performance—from theatre-goers generally and even from many (though of course not all) the devoted admirers of *Carmen* in its original form. The real test was in the number of

120

CHANGING the locale of Merimée's *Carmen* from a Spanish cigarette factory to a parachute plant in the southern United States necessitated also a change in motivation, speech and stress. Fortunately for the theatre, for Bizet's music (not fundamentally altered) and for both the performers and the audience, the libretto for *Carmen Jones* was made by a man of taste, talent and experience, Oscar Hammerstein II. With fresh, young, gifted singers the production rewarded the venture.

people who came away saying, "After the first half-hour I forgot that the actors were Negroes." Robeson had dominated the stage as Othello, a Moor; in *Carmen Jones,* conversely, race was not an issue. The unknown actors had made their mark; they were living characters in a fascinating play made of words that sang, words that were well sung to Bizet's alluring music. It was another milestone passed toward the goal where the path of the Negro theatre would no longer be a separate road.

There are several names in that list of *Carmen Jones* actors that are much better known today, and one thing that helped the singers through a brilliant but trying experience was that a double cast had been trained for the important roles in order that fresh young voices might not be worn down. Muriel Smith and Muriel Rahn alternated as Carmen; Luther Saxon and Napoleon Reed as Joe (Don José); Carlotta Franzell and Elton Warren as Cindy Lou (Micaela). Glenn Bryant played Husky Miller (Escamillo), the prize fighter, and Cosy Cole beat wonderful rhythms on a wonderful drum.

Not every Negro presentation around this time had the same good fortune that *Othello* had or *Carmen Jones,* but neither were Negro shows alone in their Broadway misfortunes. *Hollywood Pinafore,* with a book by George Kaufman, and with Victor Moore and William Gaxton to enliven it, had as little success as another *Pinafore* variant called *Memphis Bound* that had an all-Negro cast including Bill Robinson, Avon Long and Frank Wilson. Broadway was playing fast and loose with so many things that you could not be sure what combination an audience would want. But in the meantime things were still moving forward; it had come to be a part of the newer musical comedy formula to have at least one Negro feature—a dancing star, a chorus line, a singer, or sometimes all three. *On the Town* handled a mixed chorus with unusual success. Almost every important musical in the forties turned somehow, someplace, toward the Negro actor and, as in *Bloomer Girl,* for example, much to the show's advantage, with Dooley Wilson as Pompey, singing "The Eagle and Me," and Richard Huey, a very old hand at this sort of thing, singing "I Got a Song" in the folk tradition.

A new impulse had also developed, perhaps as an end-product of the Federal Theatre. It showed up first in the organization of a Negro Playwrights Company whose purpose was "to foster the spirit of unity between races, provide an outlet for the creative talents of Negro artists . . . and supply the community with . . . theatre reflecting the historical

122

AN ESPECIALLY lively moment in Irving Berlin's wartime show *This Is the Army*. James A. Cross and William Wyckoff in a dance routine much like those that enlivened many of the shows produced at the front, in the camps and hospitals by U.S.O. Camp Shows.

PEARL PRIMUS, a young dancer and choreographer of unusual talent and a technical range that extends far beyond Negro forms and rhythms.

reality of the life of the Negro people." Among its active members were Theodore Browne, author of *Natural Man,* Theodore Ward, author of *Big White Fog,*—both Federal Theatre productions, one in Seattle and one in Chicago—Langston Hughes, already widely known both as poet and dramatist, and Owen Dodson, rapidly coming to the fore through the productions of his group at the Great Lakes Naval Training Station. *Big White Fog,* with which the company opened, provided a new and welcome setting for Negro drama, the home of an educated middle-class Chicago family.

Soon afterwards, another organization appeared on the scene, putting on plays in a tiny basement theatre in the 135th Street Library in Harlem and, at the same time, working hard training players, directors and technicians. This was the American Negro Theatre, directed by Abram Hill, himself a playwright, author of *On Striver's Row.* The group had energy, talent, a fighting spirit and an active sense of what made the news. The General Education Board of the Rockefeller Foundation recognized the value of the organization and its work by a generous award, and before long the record showed what could be done.

A play called *Anna Lucasta* had been hawked around among New York producers, had aroused some interest, but never made a sale. The author was a young Chicagoan, Philip Yordan. It was concerned, in its original form, with a low-class Polish family in a Pennsylvania industrial town—their personal, social and economic relationships and what effects these had on their lives. To the many unpleasant complications inherent in the characters and the story were added overtones of broad comedy and of "social significance."

Claire Leonard, agent for the play, suggested to Abram Hill, director of the American Negro Theatre, that he adapt it for his company's use. Hill did this, and put it on in Harlem under Harry Wagstaff Gribble's direction. Several Broadway critics saw the play, recognized the vigor of the dialogue and the sharp character drawing, were pleased to find a new dramatic talent, and gave the play more attention than off-Broadway productions usually receive. *Anna Lucasta* was brought downtown by John Wildberg where it continued for 956 performances. Two off-Broadway companies were formed and one of them played 44 weeks in Chicago before it went to California; a second played many weeks in Philadelphia and other Eastern cities. Hilda Simms as Anna, Frederick O'Neal, one of the founders of the American Negro Theatre, as her

HILDA SIMMS as Anna, Hubert Henry and Alvin Childress in *Anna Lucasta,* as produced on Broadway by John Wildberg. Originally about a Polish family, Philip Yordan's play was given its first showing by Abram Hill and his experimental American Negro Theatre in a Harlem library basement. Acclaimed by several critics, it was brought downtown with many from the original cast and became a long-lived hit. With two companies on the road, it has played over 300 weeks.

brother Frank, and several other members of the cast promptly made names for themselves.

Anna Lucasta made another dent in the theatre's weakening fences. Here, again, was a drama that had nothing fundamental to do with race and again the audience accepted the Negro cast as actors, as they had accepted the singing-actors of *Carmen Jones.* And, almost immediately, the success of the play encouraged the production of others based on some of the more serious aspects of life, plays like *Deep Are the Roots, Strange Fruit, Jeb.* None of these plays was in the poet's line, like *Porgy* or *Green Pastures,* but in the line of *Stevedore* and *Native Son.* They were of varying quality and met a varying fate but it was obvious that the Negro *material* itself was beginning to count for its human and social, as well as its literary value.

Deep Are the Roots was an early season offering by Arnaud d'Usseau and James Gow, staged by Elia Kazan. It was a product of the war, like the authors' earlier play *Tomorrow the World.* In place of the young Nazi who was the villain of the earlier piece there were certain unreconstructed American fascists.

The play's protagonist was a young Negro officer, the well-educated son of a trusted servant in the home of a Southern senator. When Lt. Brett Charles came home full of war's honors he was eager to accept an offer to teach in the Negro village school. But the Senator's older daughter, who prides herself on her broad-mindedness and who has helped the boy in many ways, has other plans for him. She has secured a scholarship at a Northern university and resents Brett's making his own plans. The plot thickens fast, in the best melodramatic tradition, and when the younger sister, Genevra Langdon, Brett's childhood playmate, invites him to take her for an evening walk and the news spreads— growing as it goes on—that is all that is needed to "frame" the young man for the theft of a watch. A romantic scene with little sister boldly showing her devotion, the theft cleared up, and little sister packing her valise and heading North in revolt, make the major elements of the play. It is easy to give it a machine-made sound, and certainly it is more old-fashioned in its method than in its basic idea. But the authors are good builders and writers of good dialogue, as well as high-spirited journalists. As played, *Deep Are the Roots* was effective both as theatre and as argument, which the authors intended that it should be. For the young lieutenant, played with poise and deep earnestness by Gordon

Heath, was one of the men who have earned a new dignity in the war that we will not have them deprived of, now that the war is over and the old fight begun. The reactionary senator was too much like certain legislators who are making life miserable for all of us today to have us bear with him easily. The older sister, the insistent and inflexible reformer-within-bounds, was too well played by Carol Goodner not to arouse our antagonism. And Barbara Geddes, who created the part of Genevra Langdon, carried it off with such faith, fire and beauty that every audience stood with her. Admitting all the limitations of *Deep Are the Roots,* you were glad that it was one of the season's successes.

By the same token you could not help regretting the failure of *Strange Fruit* and *Jeb* to find an audience to listen with sympathy to the problems they presented, even though one might well ask what gave them any right to more attention than other failures. Why bother about plays that don't come off in the theatre—even if they are sincere and their material is fresh and indubitably dramatic—if, as we insist, the theatre is not a forum, not a pulpit, not a journal, but an art whose intrinsic values must be respected if it is to maintain its power?

The answer is that the theatre, like all art, needs fresh material with each new age, and needs each age's fresh way of handling its material. This seems to create an inconsistency between the practices of our commercial theatre and the theatre's best interests. In a permanent theatre where plays and playwrights can mature slowly some new material can be added each year, like fresh soil in a garden, and can be reworked until it becomes part of the native soil. But in our theatre, where seventy-five percent of all plays fail, fresh material is seldom absorbed. And if we do not learn from our worthy failures we do not learn at all.

Jeb, by Robert Ardrey, was another post-war play and was, in certain ways, a better one than *Deep Are the Roots.* Its idea was clearer and more defined; it kept the action well within the frame of that idea. It was, again, the story of a soldier going back to an unreconstructed South that was, to him, a home he loved. He came without honors and minus a leg, but with something new that seemed wonderful to him. This was the trade the Army had taught him, making him an expert operator of an adding machine. But the leading citizens of the town will not accept the idea of a Negro in a white man's job, and, gradually, the antagonism which presses upon Jeb almost makes him doubt his

128

own capacity. He gathers strength enough to break into the office to test himself. But just as his skilful fingers make the keys hum the time-keeper finds him. He is beaten, driven out of town, his home is burned. Robert Ardrey does not try to find the solution for the whole problem of social economic rivalry, but he meets Jeb's problem squarely. Jeb goes North, but only to strengthen his will to come back and fight it out on his own home line. Ossie Davis, who played Jeb Turner, and Jeb himself, will not be forgotten.

Lillian Smith's famous novel, *Strange Fruit,* had nothing to do with the events or effects of World War II. Its warfare was the older strife of races in the South. The characters and incidents of the story were so dramatic that it seemed inevitable that the novel should be made into a play. But Lillian Smith and her sister, who dramatized it, made the mistake of trying to recreate—within the range of a single stage and one evening's playing time—both the whole of her central story and almost all of the book's luminous and varicolored background. The acting and direction were good; but *Strange Fruit* on the stage was not a play, it was a panorama of rural life in Georgia.

Democratic consciousness, in America, has developed in the last half-century to a point where both the finest players and their audiences are mature enough to wrestle with the same problems that make our major political, economic and racial conflicts. But a play cannot always find its audience as quickly as present Broadway economics demand. Success is still too often an accident of news value or of brilliant acting; failure is too often due to a poor start, to theatre inexperience, to wordiness or too much scene-shifting, or to trying to do more than the play-form can profitably hold.

Yet anyone who knows and understands Broadway's own problems and the enormous handicaps under which even the best of its workers labor day by day knows that, if such a complex, centralized theatre is to continue to exist, everybody concerned in its survival—theatre owners, producers, artists and craftsmen—must hope to make money. And he knows, too, that in a great many ways the Broadway theatre has been more generous to its artists than most theatres. It is within this frame-work that—today—we must face the playwright's problem although we may well look forward to other, and better, days.

If, on the surface, this looks like a stalemate the events of the very next season show how unwise it is to predict what the wise old theatre

CAMILLA WILLIAMS won critical acclaim for her singing of the name part in the New York City Center production of *Madame Butterfly*. Here a year earlier Todd Duncan had distinguished himself in *Pagliacci*.

MILDRED SMITH and Alfred Drake in *Beggar's Holiday,* a modern version of Gay's immortal *Beggar's Opera* and an example of Negro-white collaboration in the theatre. For it Duke Ellington set John Latouche's lyrics to music to make his first major contribution to the Broadway theatre. The principals were Negro and white, as were the leading dancers and the chorus. Even the producing team—Oliver Smith, who also designed the sets, and Perry Watkins—and the orchestra demonstrated the same inter-racial cooperation.

131

will do, and can do, when it is important to adjust itself to the age in which it lives. And how it does, in fact, learn even from unsuccess.

In the Spring of '46 Canada Lee, heretofore known to the theatre only as an actor, appeared in the role of co-producer for a play on race relations called *On Whitman Avenue*, by Maxine Wood. A little later he pioneered again when he played, in white-face, the difficult role of DeBosola in Webster's *Duchess of Malfi*, in a production which not even the presence of Elisabeth Bergner could bring to life. *Lysistrata* was the next entrant; it had an all Negro cast which was used to no particular advantage. Up to this point things looked more adventurous than happy. But soon the tide turned: Camilla Williams made a brilliant appearance as Madame Butterfly with the City Center Opera Company, where Todd Duncan had come off with flying colors as Canio in *Pagliacci* the year before. Katherine Dunham, with her growing company of dancing and singing actors, presented what is acknowledged to be by far her best show, the *Bal Nègre*. Frank Marriott found favor in the role of a Negro gambler in O'Neill's *The Iceman Cometh*. Duke Ellington brought his skill to the service of the theatre with the score for *Beggar's Holiday*, a modern version of *The Beggar's Opera*, to which audiences responded eagerly in spite of the fact that the music and lyrics were not always well matched, and that Alfred Drake, one of the best of our musical comedy singers, lacked enough sinister quality to focus either the character of Macheath or the social impact of the original play. The performance was enriched by the glowing and mobile settings of Oliver Smith, Avon Long's dancing, Mildred Smith's charm, and a spirited mixed chorus of dancers and singers. Perry Watkins, who had gained his spurs as the designer of the Federal Theatre *Pinocchio* and of Guthrie McClintic's production of *Mamba's Daughters*, was co-producer of the elaborate show. *Street Scene*, the musical version of Elmer Rice's drama, with music by Kurt Weill, had lyrics by Langston Hughes that combined the street's vernacular and Hughes' free and rambling rhythms with the spirit of the music to excellent effect. On the heels of these successes, doubling on their use of a mixed Negro and white cast, came the delightful fantasy, *Finian's Rainbow*, to provide new anchor to our hopes.

So about all that remains of the dreaded stalemate lies in the undoubted fact that Broadway still offers little opportunity for playwrights—any playwrights—to learn how to handle new dramatic

132

IN *FINIAN'S RAINBOW*, a satiric fantasy of white supremacy in the U. S. South, David Wayne (above), as an Irish leprechaun who had followed a stolen pot of gold to "Missitucky," sings to some of the charming younger members of the cast. Like their elders in both the singing and dancing choruses, they are Negro and white. The chorus of the musical version of *Street Scene* (below) likewise blends Negro and white voices.

material successfully, or to try out the new skills it needs so badly. Everything is too hurried, too harried and much too expensive. For where, while this remains true, is there any hope for new Negro dramatists?

There is a simple answer to that question, a question that has, in fact, little to do with race. The answer will apply if playwrights—all playwrights—will learn to take their time; if they will stop looking with over-eager eyes at the fortunes rolled up by half-a-dozen hit plays a year, and count the money and time and the talents and the courage that are squandered every year on Broadway failures. A wise Negro educator once said: "There is one American trait that I will never teach my boys—to hurry without knowing what they are hurrying towards." If he and his fellows will only persist in that determination Negro dramatists will learn their craft *before* they head for Broadway. For Broadway, with its human and economic complexity, the wealth of talent at its immediate disposal, its conflicting interests, its technical elaboration and invention, was never fitted to be a seedbed but might easily be the finest showshop in the whole world.

Our hopeful dramatists—all of them—might well take their cue from the record of the American Negro actors for, in numbers and in quality, no other Negro theatre group anywhere can equal them. And where did the most talented and successful among them learn their craft? Not on Broadway; not one in ten on Broadway. They learned it the hard way, in vaudeville, with the Pekin Stock Company in Chicago, the Lafayette in Harlem, or smaller, less-known organizations of that kind.

In the Who's Who of the recent playbills you find two groups. First the older players. There is Evelyn Ellis. She received her training with the Lafayette Theatre, played in Nan Stephen's *Roseanne,* was the first Bess in *Porgy,* was in *Native Son* and is Brett Charles' mother in *Deep Are the Roots.* Juano Hernandez, a street minstrel in Rio de Janeiro thirty years ago, has played in every form of theatre from showboat and honky-tonk to radio. He played at the Provincetown Playhouse, with Miller and Lyles in *Rang-Tang;* he was Sam Perry in *Strange Fruit.* Edna Thomas was a member of the Lafayette Players and the Ethiopian Art Theatre and made her Broadway debut in *Lulu Belle.* She played important parts in *Porgy, Run, Little Chillun, Stevedore,* and was Lady Macbeth in the Federal Theatre production. She was Mamie McIntosh in *Strange Fruit.*

134

IT MAY well have been a production of *Hamlet*, directed by Owen Dodson for the Hampton University Communications Theatre, that secured for Gordon Heath the leading role of Lt. Brett Charles in *Deep Are the Roots* on Broadway. Ophelia, in the Hampton production, was played by Marion Douglas, the beautiful granddaughter of two of America's leading Negro theatre artists, Will Marion Cook and his wife Abbie Mitchell.

The younger ones, lacking a training ground like the Lafayette, have turned, to their advantage, to the experimental theatres. Gordon Heath (the Lt. Brett Charles of *Deep Are the Roots*) has worked with the Richard B. Harrison Players, with the Harlem Independent Theatre, the Rose McClendon Players, the American Negro Theatre and the Communications Theatre of Hampton Institute. Several years ago "Theatre Arts Magazine" picked him as a "young hopeful" when he played Higgins in *Pygmalion* (designed and directed by Owen Dodson) at Hampton, and again when he played Hamlet there. Helen Martin (Honey Turner in *Deep Are the Roots*) is another former member of the Rose McClendon Players and of the American Negro Theatre. And so they grow, usually by slow stages, from amateur to professional.

Perhaps the most varied record, one that shows how far a man can go, if he has patience and talent and training, is that made by Frank Wilson, who began in the theatre when there were no "legitimate" Negro actors. He studied at the American Academy of Dramtic Arts and, while he was there, presented short Negro plays in Harlem and carried mail there as well. He played for years in the Lafayette and Lincoln Theatres. He had good notices in *All God's Chillun Got Wings* at the Provincetown and, many years later, played the lead in that play at the London Gate Theatre. He understudied Gilpin as The Emperor Jones and played Lem, the native chief. He succeeded Jules Bledsoe in the name part of *In Abraham's Bosom,* and through that won the part of Porgy which he played 851 times on Broadway, in London and on the road. He was Moses in *Green Pastures*, and played in *Roll, Sweet Chariot, You Can't Take It with You, Watch on the Rhine, Anna Lucasta.* He ends an account of his own record with these words: "We gave a command performance of *Watch on the Rhine* for the late President Franklin Delano Roosevelt at the National Theatre in Washington, D. C. We had dinner at the White House with the President. I sat at his table and discussed with him *Porgy and Bess,* Hitler, poison gas, Rudolph Hess and Russia." It can be done!

There is another top-notch story that must, some day, some not-too-distant day, be told in full; for the edifying comment it makes on American social and theatre history and for its illumination of the artist's spiritual dedication to his work, with or without material reward. It is not entirely a theatre story, but it crosses the theatre, happily, in many places. It is a family story that began when two graduates of Oberlin

136

MOURNING BECOMES ELECTRA at Howard University. In this production by Owen Dodson, Patricia Roberts is seen as Lavinia Mannon and Sadie Brown as Christine.

137

went to Howard University, John Cook as Professor of Law and Secretary to General O. O. Howard, and his wife as teacher of Domestic Science. Their son, Will Marion Cook, went back to Oberlin, won a scholarship to study violin with Joachim in Berlin and graduated at the head of his class. Undaunted by the discovery that Americans were not yet ready to accept a Negro as concert violinist he turned his attention to composition, determined to prove the musical value of Negro themes and rhythms. His theatre career began in 1898, with a "smash-hit," produced by George W. Lederer, *Clorindy: The Origin of the Cakewalk* (lyrics by Paul Laurence Dunbar). He wrote most of the music for the Williams and Walker shows, some for the elder Hammerstein, and many popular numbers. Today his best known works are his serious choral ensembles like *Exhortation* and *Swing Along.* In 1919 he took his "Negro Syncopated Orchestra" to London where it played for nine months, and then toured. Many Negro artists—musicians, singers, composers, actors— acknowledge his influence and often his beneficent help. His wife was Abbie Mitchell, who starred in most of the shows he composed, toured Europe and America with great success as a concert artist, (See page 36), became leading dramatic and operatic artist of the Lafayette Theatre, and is still playing roles as varied as Clara, in *Porgy and Bess,* and Addie, in *The Little Foxes.* Mercer Cook, son of Abbie Mitchell and Will Marion Cook is Professor of Romance Languages at Howard; their daughter Marion, singer and dancer, married Lewis Douglas who made his theatre reputation chiefly in Europe, as dancer, choreographer and director. He played with Max Reinhardt and with Ufa Films and directed the *Revue Nègre* which presented Josephine Baker to Paris. It is Douglas' daughter who, to round out the theatre picture, is seen as Ophelia to Gordon Heath's Hamlet in the Hampton production. (Page 135.) Yes, it can be done.

Many Negro members of Equity have today about the same wretched percentage of opportunity to earn a living that other actors have; which is, on the average, the chance of a few weeks' work a year. That is not a happy prospect, to be sure, but at least it is not a problem of race but of the unsound basis on which our theatre is organized. It does not alter the fact that, among the Negro actors who have made good, those that were well trained have had the best results, and that they got their training before they met the tough professional competition of Broadway.

138

THE GILPIN PLAYERS of the Karamu Theatre in Cleveland have sent more than a score of fine players, singers and dancers to the professional stage. Under the leadership of Russell and Rowena Jelliffe they have produced well over a hundred plays, many of them original scripts of Negro life. Before their tiny theatre burned down Langston Hughes always found a welcome for his refreshing dramas, like the comedy *When the Jack Hollers* (above), written in collaboration with Arna Bontemps. (Below) The sketch for a new and better-equipped Karamu Theatre.

Surely, if actors can do it playwrights with as much talent *and patience* can do it too. All the signs point to the fact that, for many Negro playwrights, the solution of their problem is to learn their craft in The Tributary Theatre where—for all American playwrights—the hope has lain, largely neglected, for a generation. Whatever happy fancy imagination may release to an experienced pen, surely a young playwright should write first out of his experience of life, of the things and the people he knows. He should be close to his material, where the way of life, the idioms of language, the rhythms of speech and gesture and movement will flow, naturally, to the surface of his writing. Above all—if he is to grow to his full stature—he should not be subject to a thousand theatre clichés, to the irrational demands of theatre capital and theatre labor, until his writing has matured.

The Negroes have made good beginnings in their Tributary Theatres against heavy odds—at Howard, at Spelman, at Talledega, at Hampton and many other places. At the Karamu Theatre in Cleveland the Gilpin Players under the direction of Russell and Rowena Jelliffe had produced over one hundred manuscript plays, many of them of Negro life, before their tiny theatre burned down a few years ago. They had developed a dance group and a chorus that were known all over the country and today over a score of their players and dancers are on Broadway or in Broadway companies on the road. Their plans for a new and better theatre are ready; they have, with endless labor, raised all the money that would have been necessary to build it if prices had not mounted so high since the estimates were made. The cost of a single Broadway failure would still make their theatre possible if only some Broadway "angel" had imagination enough to envisage the return from that investment. But the Jelliffes and their group are not discouraged; they are waiting, and while they wait they are producing again, in a hall, with the audience on four sides.

Even the tiny Bucket Theatre, seven miles from Tuskegee, that started, hopefully, just before the war, may well serve as a symbol for the hope ahead. It got its name from a story, now familiar, told by Booker T. Washington in his famous speech at the Atlanta Exposition in 1895, that became the keynote of Negro progress in education and in industry. A number of sailors, Mr. Washington said, were adrift off the coast of South America. They were suffering desperately from thirst when suddenly a steamer came within hailing range. The sailors sig-

140

PEARL BAILEY, a talented member of the younger generation in the theatre, as Butterfly in *St. Louis Woman* (1946), her first good opportunity on Broadway. The musical was written by Countee Cullen and Arna Bontemps, music by Vernon Duke, and with Ruby Hill in a leading role.

nalled for water and the answer came: "Cast down your buckets where you are." They did as they were told and drew up fresh water for they had drifted into the wide mouth of the Amazon.

The extension division of Tuskegee made the little Bucket Theatre for farmers who had no other opportunity for recreation and amusement. Carrying their hoes and their hammers with them after their day's work, they remade a dilapidated store under Saunders Walker's direction. They laid a new floor, made a new stage, painted the building inside and out with paints made for them in Dr. George Washington Carver's laboratory. The Negro farmers were not only the audience for the plays. They helped in the staging and they were the actors. Many of the plays, written for them at Tuskegee, were about the life these farmers knew, and there was a bond between actors and audience that many big playhouses may well envy. In fact, in spite of the storm he created when he suggested that "there is as much dignity in tilling a field as in writing a poem," Booker Washington may well have provided a text for the entire American Tributary Theatre of the next generation: "Cast down your buckets where you are."

In the meantime another dream may come true, a dream no more impossible than such an institution as Tuskegee and such a laboratory as Dr. Carver's must have seemed to Booker Washington in 1895. For, if the charter for a National Theatre is ever really activated, as it can and should be, we will have theatres across the land that can serve all our actors, directors, singers, dancers and playwrights as seed bed and harvest.

N. Y. CRITICS who went down to the Henry Street Playhouse (formerly the Neighborhood Playhouse) to see *Our Lan'* by Theodore Ward, author of *Big White Fog,* came back moved and enthusiastic. A saga of hope betrayed, it concerns the post-Civil War struggle of freed slaves to retain the land given them. *Our Lan'* was produced by the Associated Playwrights and played with conviction by Negro actors led by Muriel Smith and William Veasey.